# THE POWER OF REALISTIC THINKING

## How to Cope When How-to Books Fail

# Donald W. McCullough

author of *Finding Happiness in the Most Unlikely Places*

INTERVARSITY PRESS
DOWNERS GROVE, ILLINOIS 60515

© 1988 by Donald W. McCullough

Originally published under the title Waking from the American Dream.

All rights reserved. No part of this book may be reproduced in any form without written permission from InterVarsity Press, P.O. Box 1400, Downers Grove, IL 60515.

InterVarsity Press is the book-publishing division of InterVarsity Christian Fellowship, a student movement active on campus at hundreds of universities, colleges and schools of nursing in the United States of America, and a member movement of the International Fellowship of Evangelical Students. For information about local and regional activities, write Public Relations Dept., InterVarsity Christian Fellowship, 6400 Schroeder Rd., P.O. Box 7895, Madison, WI 53707-7895.

All Scripture quotations, unless otherwise indicated, are from the Revised Standard Version of the Bible, copyrighted 1946, 1952, 1971, by the Division of Christian Education of the National Council of the Churches of Christ in the U.S.A., and are used by permission.

ISBN 0-8308-1311-X

Printed in the United States of America ∞

**Library of Congress Cataloging-in-Publication Data**

McCullough, Donald W., 1949-
    [Waking from the American dream]
    The power of realistic thinking: how to cope when how-to books
fail/Donald W. McCullough.
       p.      cm.
    Originally published: Waking from the American dream. Downers
Grove, Ill.: InterVarsity Press, c1988.
    Includes bibliographical references.
    ISBN 0-8308-1311-X
    1. Christian life—1960-    I. Title.
BV4501.2.M2235    1992
248.4—dc20                  92-5675
                                   CIP

| 17 | 16 | 15 | 14 | 13 | 12 | 11 | 10 | 9 | 8 | 7 | 6 | 5 | 4 | 3 | 2 | 1 |
|----|----|----|----|----|----|----|----|----|----|----|----|----|----|----|----|----|
| 05 | 04 | 03 | 02 | 01 | 00 | 99 | 98 | 97 | 96 | 95 | 94 | 93 | 92 | | | |

*To my parents,*
*John and Ione McCullough*

## Acknowledgments

The writing of this book was not a solitary project. I had the help of a team of people who believed in me and in the need to communicate this message. I'm grateful for those who read and offered suggestions on all or part of the chapters in draft form: Steve Carlton, Carol Dew, Tom Erickson, Mary Graves, Jim Hancock, Susan and Bill Hoehn, Jan LaBar, Joan Leeger, Alan Lewis, Ione and John McCullough, Shari and Ken Regan, and Mel Willard—good friends, all, and colleagues in the work of the kingdom. Marlene Dominy provided outstanding secretarial help. A writer couldn't hope for a better editor than Michael Maudlin of InterVarsity Press; his encouragement strengthened my spirit, even as his editing polished my prose. I would also like to thank Lori Davis for helping to develop the discussion questions. Finally, I want to thank my wife, Karen, and my daughters, Jennifer and Joy, for their constant love and support.

# D R E A M I N G

You don't know quite
what it is you do want,
but it just fairly
makes your heart ache
you want it so.
*MARK TWAIN*

# CHAPTER ONE

# When Can-Do Can't

**G**ood *stories are true; they illustrate with particular circumstances,* whether factual or fictional, the truths we all live through in one way or another. The reason for telling a story, as William Faulkner once observed, is to illuminate "the ageless, eternal struggle" of being human. The stories of Jim Waldal and Mary Sayers focus a light on part of the conflict in which we find ourselves—the struggle between our dreams and the inevitable reality that overtakes them.

**Jim Waldal**
Jim was raised on Queen Anne hill, a middle-class neighborhood

in Seattle, by parents who provided a stable, loving environment. His mother was generous and gregarious, and his father incarnated the virtues of the American work ethic. Though completing only seven grades of formal education, Thor Waldal had achieved much, rising to the position of general manager of a steamship line and to the rank of captain in the Navy Reserve.

Thor proclaimed the gospel of hard work and extolled the virtues of education and financial independence. And Jim practiced what was preached: he played basketball, studied diligently, achieved ranking in the "top ten" of his high-school class and eventually entered the University of Washington for the college education his father had planned for him.

But during his freshman year Jim spent more time socializing than studying and nearly flunked out. This created a crisis at home. "It was the only time my father violently disciplined me," Jim recalled. "He was so mad he had tears in his eyes. He knew I had failed because I didn't try."

The confrontation brought Jim back to the straight and narrow road of hard work. He settled down to the task of earning a degree and a commission in the Navy through the Reserve Officer Training Corps. He enjoyed school but hated the engineering major he was advised to pursue by counselors impressed with his mathematical skills. What really interested him was business. He dreamed of financial independence—owning a company, being a millionaire before he turned forty, succeeding like the young men he read about in *Barrons*.

So after graduation he went to the Navy Supply Corps School to learn business. Graduating sixth in a class of 186 gave him the opportunity to choose his place of duty. Understandably, he chose Hawaii. But Jim gained more than a suntan out of his Navy experience; he improved his leadership and organizational skills.

Those skills continued to mature after his Navy discharge. He enrolled again at the University of Washington, earning another B.A. and an M.A., joined the faculty for a year, and in June of 1964 became the western region sales representative for National Lead Industries. The office was based in Los Angeles, and so Jim took his new bride, Ellie, to "the land of opportunity."

He was offered higher paying jobs, but the one he chose had other compensations: his travels enabled him to observe firsthand dozens of successful industries, and this broad exposure proved a well-placed steppingstone toward the achievement of his dreams. He wanted to start a company, to create something of significance, to "build an empire."

Gathering together these dreams and all the capital he could scrape up, Jim joined four others in 1971 to establish Viclan, a company making multi-layered chip capacitors. This was risky, a throw of the dice at a time when he might have been more concerned about buttressing his family's security (by now Jim and Ellie had three children to support); they had every reason to stay put, to sink roots deeply in the soil of their comfortable suburban life. But believing that only those willing to risk much can gain much, Jim mortgaged everything—even his furniture—and eventually moved his family to San Diego, the site chosen for the fledgling company. Severing ties with a much-loved church and a large network of friends created great stress for the family, and Jim acknowledged that Ellie's willingness to move demonstrated "true love on her part."

The risk-taking was not over. In 1976 Jim's other partners wanted out of the business. That left him with two difficult questions to answer. *Should* he buy out his partners and put his family's security on the line again? *Could* he buy out his partners? Where would he find enough money to make the deal? As always, Ellie was supportive, ready to share the risks. And maybe that was all the security he needed.

Jim mustered the troops—his goal of financial independence, the hard-work philosophy of his father, the can-do spirit of his American heritage and his faith in God—for one last march toward the fulfillment of his dreams. He mortgaged his house again, begged and borrowed every dime he could, and somehow found funds to buy the company. He hoped to enlarge it enough to sell at a profit and then move on to something else.

It worked.

Less than two years later the company had tripled in size, and he sold it to a Japanese firm for "megabucks," to use his word. His dream had come true. "I was at the top of my world," Jim said. "We had all the money we would want. I had achieved what I set out to do. I had the world by the tail."

Things could not have been going better for Jim . . . except for one thing. He noticed he was having trouble tying his tie. Well, Jim thought, hardly anything to worry about when everything else is going your way! After all, he was now forty-one, "over the hill." So he started lifting weights. He didn't get to his position in life by falling over in the first little breeze that blew his way.

But some breezes, if we only knew which, gently warn of stronger winds to follow. For Jim, a typhoon was approaching.

The weakness persisted. Perhaps he needed a doctor's advice; a professional opinion couldn't hurt. It did, though. Truth can hurt; it can trounce the spirit and beat it senseless. He was told he needed another opinion, from a neurologist. And the neurologist's opinion was this: "Jim, you have a disease of the anterior horn cells. You have A.L.S.—Lou Gehrig's disease. You've got three years to live, seven at the outside. Sell your house and take a vacation."

It was unbelievable, literally. Disbelief is the first arrow drawn from the quiver of self-defense when an unfriendly future advances against us. But its range is limited, its force soon spent. Within a few days Jim was reaching for the second arrow—anger. And who but God should receive the burden of his wrath? "What have I done?" Jim wondered. "Why me? Why am I being punished?" But this arrow, too, proves ineffective; it breaks against the impenetrable silence of God.

No answers came to set at rest his questioning mind. He was given, instead, a presence to set at peace his trembling heart—the presence of Christ. "I thought it was a dream," Jim remembered, "but it might have been a vision. I'm not sure; it doesn't matter. What happened was this: in the middle of the night my bedroom lit up and I could see the face of Jesus. His head was turned slightly, but his eyes were looking at me. At once I had a feeling of warmth, like I'd consumed a lot of brandy. I sensed his presence all around me and in me. Then I woke up. Or maybe I had been awake. In any event, I was changed."

His physical condition, however, didn't change. But the disease couldn't reach into his spirit. The contrast between diseased body and vibrant personality would often startle others. More than a few discovered, in Jim's presence, courage and a new faith in God.

Jim continued to pray for healing and believed, without a hint of doubt, that he would be healed. His only question was, "Will God heal me before or after I stop breathing?" Either way, wholeness would be his—whether in this life or the next—and this confidence filled him with peace.

He had concerns, of course. He worried about the burden on his family; he wondered whether he would see his son's high-school graduation; he struggled with whether to go on a respirator when the disease started attacking his lungs; he feared the pain which might accompany his dying—these things made lonely days and long nights difficult. Yet he had this: the presence of God. "God is with me," he said, "I have no fear of death."

A.L.S. robbed Jim of many things, finally even his life. But even as God used evil kings of Babylon to refine his people in the furnace of holy love, so also he used disease to remake Jim into a better person. Almost all Jim's values changed before he died. His goals, for example, went through a death and resurrection. He still wanted to achieve, only he had a radically different standard for success. He told me, "I used to think achievement meant being president of a company and being surrounded by signs of material success; now I know achievement means pleasing God and serving others."

Another significant change for Jim was in his relationship with his children. "Before, I was too strict," he admitted. "But now the children see how much I need them. There is more give and take on both sides. I'm more compassionate and patient."

Jim would have been the first to acknowledge he wasn't ready for canonization. He struggled with some things until his death, as everyone does. And yet clearly God used something evil in itself, a horrible disease, to bring about a conversion. To convert means to turn around, and that exactly describes what happened to Jim. "Before I became sick," he said, "I believed in God. I wasn't a bad person, really. I didn't cheat or use drugs or do those sorts of things. But my life was based on my desires. Now my life is based on God's desires." And this profession he proved by the way he died. His suffering and brokenness were present at the end, certainly, but so was complete trust in the final healing awaiting him.

## Mary Sayers

As Mary shared with me some of her recent experiences as a small group leader in our church, my thoughts wandered back a few years to a very different conversation.[1] We were seated in the sunny courtyard of a local mental hospital. Her psychiatrist, suspecting a spiritual side to her struggles, had suggested she talk with her pastor. So I went and listened and heard a broken, guilt-ridden woman trying to fit puzzling pieces of a life into a meaningful picture. She cried in pain and laughed in scorn; she thanked me for coming and hated my presence; she talked wildly and sat quietly; she hungered for God and denied his existence. She was in the pit—or so it seemed.

In truth, she was on the path toward power. Julien Green, describing the conversion of St. Francis, wrote, "For years he had been fleeing someone or something, and suddenly that someone had caught up with him and blasted him with all the power of his tenderness."[2] Mary was experiencing the blast of God's grace, the severe side of his mercy; she was being transformed into the person she is today.

Mary has virtually no warm memories of her childhood. Instead, she remembers living in constant fear of her older brother. He had had high expectations placed on him following their father's premature death, and a boy cannot step into a man's shoes without some ill-fitting consequences. His frustrations turned to anger, and his anger turned toward Mary. Words wounded her pride, blows bruised her body, and more important, the continual abuse laid waste her self-esteem.

The first time she felt she was perhaps worth more than a punching bag came at the age of fifteen. A friend named Bill had undergone a conversion experience through Youth for Christ and was on fire to save anyone who came along. "I came along," she says. "I feared God's judgment and wanted to do something fast before the ax fell." Bill got her involved in his church, and it became a new world for her, a place for spiritual growth and the development of latent leadership skills she never knew she had. Her self-esteem was beginning to get up out of the dirt.

When the time came to choose a college, one institution had a distinct advantage over all the others—the one Bill had started attending two years earlier. They were still "just friends," but very friendly friends indeed. Praying about it together convinced them that God wanted her to follow Bill and enroll in the denomination's missionary college. But Mary's growing attachment to Bill was not the only factor in the decision. She wanted to serve God and dreamed of becoming a missionary in New Guinea.

A romance with Bill ripened rapidly in the sunlight of constant contact. By November they were engaged; in December, during Christmas break, they were married; a year later they had their first child.

Stephen's birth went smoothly, but about three weeks later the pediatrician detected some irregularities in his reflexes. Specialists eventually confirmed what the pediatrician had suspected. Stephen had Down's syndrome, a congenital condition characterized by moderate to severe mental deficiency, compounded by a serious heart defect. There were frequent hospitalizations for pneumonia and heart failure. It was, of course, a difficult time. "I had a lot of guilt," Mary remembers, "feelings of heavy responsibility, feelings of inadequacy related to his care."

Mary and Bill turned to family and school for prayer and support. They received the prayer without the support. The explicit words addressed to God were only part of the messages conveyed in prayers on behalf of Stephen. There were others, implicit but none-theless clearly communicated, directed to Bill and Mary: perhaps this resulted from getting married so young; perhaps their faith needed strengthening; perhaps they had unconfessed sin. The col-lege president's wife, for example, once went to the hospital to visit Mary and Stephen, and happened to arrive during one of Mary's infrequent respites from her bedside vigil. So the woman wrote Mary a note in which she recalled sitting with her own sick child, and how she found it a wonderful opportunity to commune with God, and how the child recovered once she got herself right with God.

Bill actively rebelled against the atmosphere of condemnation and easy answers; he verbalized his disgust with narrow thinking; he wrote papers challenging the school's theological positions; he decided to go to a more liberal seminary after graduation.

Mary, however, responded passively, accepting more readily what people were saying. So she cranked up her spirituality and prayed and prayed and prayed. Nothing happened. At least, Stephen wasn't healed. Did it mean there was something wrong with her faith? Did it mean she wasn't praying with enough fervor? The guilt grew.

In order not to jeopardize their son's medical care by moving to another state, Bill and Mary decided to postpone seminary for a year. Stephen's doctor had recommended a new surgical procedure, and though it involved some risk, the operation seemed worth trying.

Mary felt the expected emotional crosscurrents as they wheeled Stephen into the operating room—anxiety, hope, love. But as they wheeled him out, one surging emotion swept away all others—a sense of panic and helplessness. The moment Mary saw him come off the elevator she knew something was wrong. The nurses didn't realize it until they got him to his room, and then a whirlwind of emergency activity blew Mary out of the room and onto the sidelines. Through the slightly open door, she watched Stephen's little body bounce to the jolt of the fibrillator. She knew it was no use. She knew he was dead.

Prayer was Mary's natural reflex. But, like circling vultures, questions also appeared: Does God hear my prayer? Where is divine help when I need it? Did Stephen go through all his suffering just to die?

"I began to think," says Mary, "that maybe God wasn't there to hear me. Two days after Stephen died I had a terrible dream. Someone had stolen his body and thrown it on the floor of his room. And with that image came this thought: that's all there is. With Stephen's death came another death—the death of my faith."

Bill and Mary drifted into a very different lifestyle, and for about a year it provided an enjoyable escape from the emotional devastation they had gone through. Both took jobs in New York City, which enabled them to enjoy the theater and other cultural opportunities. Eventually, however, they each began drifting in divergent directions. Bill let himself be sucked into the whirlpool of the social turmoil of the sixties; he wanted to live for the moment, to develop an "open marriage" sexually and to experiment with drugs. Mary was uncomfortable with these things. Bill was no longer the man she had married. They agreed on a separation which soon proved to be the first stage of a divorce.

They had not seen each other for some time, their marriage being clearly over, when Mary suffered another great trauma. Bill told her that mutual friends had invited them to their summer cabin. Would she go with him? She did not want to be around Bill, but this particular couple had been very supportive during the time of Stephen's illness and death. So for their sake she went.

It was a setup. Bill had lied. Their friends weren't coming. He wanted something from her badly enough to lie, badly enough to take it by force. When Mary remembers the incident today, her head hangs, not with shame, for she was a victim, but with pain, with the weight of remembered violation and humiliation.

And the sorrow was not over: she became pregnant.

Mary had an abortion. Under the circumstances it seemed the best thing to do. Her marriage was over; she was starting a new career in the education of disabled children; she had drifted away from Christian moorings into the wider waters of secular standards; and abortion, having just been legalized, was almost the "in" thing to do in her social network.

She seemed to suffer no immediate guilt. The emptying of her womb, however, created an even deeper emptiness. She began to feel the barrenness of life without God. "I couldn't be angry with God," she remembers, "because I didn't believe in God. I said to myself, 'There is no God. There is no goodness in us.' I felt utter despair."

What do you do in a situation like that? You seize what good you can find. You make the best of your circumstances. That's what Mary did, throwing herself enthusiastically into her studies, establishing new friends. Academic and social successes readied her for a new life. She fell in love again, this time with a nuclear engineer who had recently been deserted by his alcoholic wife.

Mary had high hopes: she would create for Robert and his two sons a loving, supportive environment. It began with family outings and trips with Robert on his international work assignments. They were not married, but that mattered little to them—until she became pregnant. This time abortion was not even considered. Mary and Robert looked forward to their child's birth, and almost as part of the preparation for it, they were married.

A healthy baby boy was like dessert for a fine-tasting life. Robert's new job in California made possible a comfortable lifestyle, with a nice home and interesting vacations. Mary remembers that on one of those vacations, a European trip, she wrote friends to tell them how undeserving she felt of all her blessings.

But something in Mary's past nagged her into feeling she should give her son a chance to hear about the God she wasn't too sure about, and so when Andrew reached a certain age, she took him to Sunday school. While he sat in class, she could have gone home or shopped or read in the car, but she decided instead to attend the church's worship service. A restlessness started troubling Mary, growing in intensity until it became a severe, at times immobilizing, anxiety.

This inner collapse, moreover, was worsened by a collapse in her external world. Robert grew distant. His boys, now teen-agers, started using drugs, getting in trouble with the law and even abusing Andrew.

Worse yet, Andrew was diagnosed as having cystic fibrosis, a fatal disease.

Mary felt she was losing control. Her psychiatrist recommended she become a resident patient at a mental hospital. She needed constant, closely supervised care. And this doctor wisely perceived she needed more than psycho-pharmacological treatments and analysis and counseling; he knew she needed spiritual help. So Mary called me, and I went to hold the thread from her unraveling life.

Once the thread was untangled and freed from its pattern of pain, God stitched a new masterpiece.

Today Mary is a mature Christian, secure in the love of God, radiating joy and peace. She actively serves in our church, leading a spiritual growth group, training teachers and teaching a Sunday-school class. I am particularly pleased about that last activity. My daughter attends her class, and I can think of no one I would rather have teaching my child about the Lord. (That's probably the highest compliment I can give.)

Mary didn't come to this place of inner strength because everything started going her way. Not at all. Her marriage ended in divorce. Now she lives with all the stress and loneliness of a single parent. Andrew faces an uncertain future, though at present he seems to be doing well.

What caused the change in Mary? It wasn't simply the pastoral and psychiatric care. Mary had a much greater physician of the soul with enough wisdom and love and power to provide *exactly* what she needed. God treated her. And what he did was this: he embraced her with grace. Mary felt loved by God—loved though her past rose up to accuse her, loved though guilt overwhelmed her, loved though she felt unlovely, loved though she had done nothing to deserve it, loved though she wasn't even sure the Lover existed. She discovered that when God takes hold he doesn't let go; she discovered the tenacity of divine mercy; she discovered, as did another Mary long ago, that "with God nothing will be impossible."

Mary gave in, accepted her acceptance.

Now she passionately wants to serve and obey God, but with none of the former legalistic straining for a perfect piety. She knows she doesn't have to work to impress God; she is already held by grace. And the aggressiveness of God's love has freed her to trust him even when his purposes differ from her desires.

"My friends wonder how I can maintain a single life," Mary says, "and I'm not sure; but there are times when the Bridegroom of all bridegrooms is more than sufficient. His reality surpasses all fantasies of happiness."

## Our Story

The stories of Jim Waldal and Mary Sayers differ in details but parallel in pattern. Both had dreams which they struggled to achieve, both stumbled over the reality of life's limitations and fell into a pit, and both grew into mature, attractive disciples of Jesus Christ.

Jim's ambitions were "secular." He wanted what so many of us want: material security and power. And his hard-driving can-do spirit helped him achieve much. He incarnated the American dream. Eventually, however, he crashed into an obstacle—his own mortality—and all the positive thinking in the world couldn't remove it. He experienced the brokenness of life, and this was his first step forward into a new wholeness. God met him in the pit, led him out and transformed him into a man of joy and peace.

Mary's ambitions were "spiritual." She wanted to serve God, and when trials came she struggled to triumph through the power of prayer. And no doubt this desire and its ardent faith helped strengthen her. But she learned that God's purposes don't always match human desires. She too experienced the brokenness of life, and this was her first step forward into a new wholeness. God met her in the pit, led her out and transformed her into a woman of joy and peace.

We too have ambitions. We live in a culture that tells us our dreams can be realized with enough hard work and positive thinking. But at one time or another, in one way or another, we wake up to reality. We learn, often with great pain, that we can't always have what we desperately want. Perhaps a marriage leaves us lonelier than we thought possible, or a single life feels like an inescapable prison, or sexual drives remain frustrated, or vocational advancement has been blocked, or health evades us, or God seems to have locked himself in an unresponsive heaven—disappointment comes in a variety of ways, and it can send us straight into the pit.

But as Jim and Mary discovered, God can meet us in the pit. The end of our fantasies can be the beginning of a life based on the reality of God, and that means transformation for us. Oswald Chambers once wrote:

> God disciplines us by disappointment. Life may have been going on like a torrent, then suddenly down comes a barrier of disappointment, until slowly we learn that the disappointment was his appointment. God hides his treasure in darkness, and many a radiant star that was not seen before comes out. In some lives you can see the treasure, there is a sweetness and beauty about them. You wonder where the winsome power of God came from. It came from the dark places where God revealed his sovereign will in unexpected issues. "Thou hast enlarged me when I was in distress."[3]

If Oswald Chambers is right—and I believe he is—we would do well to stop running from our disappointments in order to learn the lessons God has for us through them; we would do well to trace and study the contours of the emptiness in our hearts. Why do we feel unfulfilled in life? In the next two chapters we will examine the cultural forces which intensify these feelings by inclining us to believe all things are possible with a positive spirit and hard work. Knowing more about our dreams can help us better understand the pain of awakening to the reality of life's limits.

And eventually we *do* awake. Chapter four gives voice to the longings within us, expressing candidly the disappointments we experience. Some may find this chapter pessimistic; most, I think, will be relieved to know others go through similar experiences.

What happens when we awaken to life's limits? We try, always unsuccessfully, to find means of escape, the most common being materialism, power and religion. Chapter five considers these primal temptations, these false gods who imperiously claim our loyalties but cannot save.

Only the God revealed in Jesus Christ is big enough to save. He alone can deliver from the self-centeredness intensifying our hungers, for he alone has power enough to lift us out of ourselves. Chapters six and seven show how God is much more than we think we want, but for that reason just what we need. And what we need is this: to be loved, to be held by hands that will never let us go. Because "God is love" (1 Jn 4:16), we are set free for what I call the Saturday life.

We live between Good Friday and Easter Sunday (and we will explore what this entails in the remaining chapters of the book). Being this side of the crucifixion of Jesus Christ, we live in the freedom of grace and the joy of companionship; our self-centeredness has been forgiven; and we have a Presence with us even in our worst, most godforsaken suffering. But the healing of our brokenness and the fulfillment of our deepest longing will not be ours until the morrow, until Sunday, the day of resurrection. So in the meantime we live with faith in the grace of Good Friday and hope in the deliverance of Easter.

## Discussion Questions

1. Jim Waldal was stricken with A.L.S. in his prime. How do you think his life preceding the disease prepared him for dealing with it? Were you surprised by any aspect of Jim's reaction or eventual resolution of the situation? Explain.

2. How do you think you would react if you were told that you had a terminal

disease? What would you say to God?

3. Mary and Bill reacted differently when their son was diagnosed as having Down's syndrome: Bill felt anger and Mary, guilt. Is one response better or more legitimate than the other? Why do you think this was such a lasting crisis of faith for them?

4. What attitudes or beliefs might have motivated their friends at church to treat Mary and Bill the way they did?

5. Did you expect God to work things out differently for Jim and Mary and Bill? Why or why not?

# CHAPTER TWO

# Can-Do Culture

**M**y family periodically vacations in Seattle in order to visit relatives. It's a long drive from San Diego; hundreds of miles stretch on and on, punctuated only by stops at service stations, restaurants and motels. For our children it seems like two endless days of torture. Grandmas and grandpas and aunts and uncles and cousins are waiting for them, and their imaginations race ahead to anticipated joys. Anyone with small children knows how it goes: we're not in the car thirty minutes, and a little voice in the back seat says, "Daddy, are we there yet?" "No," I answer, "this is only San Clemente."

We are like little children with our hopes for more. We graduate from high school and ask, "Are we there yet?" Something inside tells us it's only Los Angeles. We have our first romance and ask, "Are we there yet?" It's only Bakersfield. We graduate from college and ask, "Are we there yet?" It's only Modesto. We fall in love and get married and ask, "Are we there yet?" It's only Sacramento. We have children and ask, "Are we there yet?" It's only Redding. We move into the house of our dreams and ask, "Are we there yet?" It's only Medford. We go through a mid-life depression, reach out to God in a new way, and enjoy a new experience with his Spirit, and ask, "Are we there yet?" It's only Portland.

Do we ever reach Seattle? No—not in this life. One day we shall reach that "city which is to come" (Heb 13:14), but we are not yet there. Both Scripture and human experience testify to this hard fact, and spiritual maturity requires that we learn to live with it.

A cultural influence, however, makes this difficult to accept. A dominant theme in American tradition tells us that we do not need to live with unfulfillment, that we can have Seattle in the middle of Bakersfield. And maybe because longing gets so intense some days, or unfulfillment becomes so painful, or patience stumbles like a marathoner on the twenty-sixth mile, or the flame of hope splutters too feebly against an encompassing darkness—for whatever reason, we believe it. We substitute, in place of Christian hope, the dreams of this world. Like Don Quixote, clothed in tarnished convictions and astride a nag of uncertain confidence, we're on an adventure of impossible dreams.

What aspect of American culture so powerfully influences us? Our belief in the power of positive thinking.

### Positive Thinking
My one-year-old knew the story as well as I, but that in no way

diminished her expectancy. We had our ritual. When the last bit of spaghetti had been picked out of her ears, and her bib had been retired from its brave but futile defense against the onslaught of dinner, we took our usual places on the couch. I sat by the reading light, opening the book; she snuggled her diaper-padded bottom against me, thumb and mouth rendezvousing with habitual abandon. "Train!" she would exclaim, drilling the page with a stubby finger, as if seeing the picture for the first time.

The starting signal thus given, I would tell again the story we both knew so well. A train chugged and puffed along the tracks, happy because she carried such a jolly load: her cars were filled with good things for the boys and girls on the other side of the mountain. But suddenly she jerked to a stop; something was wrong, her wheels unable to turn. What were the children on the other side of the mountain going to do without the wonderful toys and good food she carried? A shiny passenger train roared by, but he was much too important to be bothered with the problems of a broken-down engine. And soon a big, strong freight train came rumbling down the tracks, but he too was busy with very weighty matters. And then came an old rusty engine, whose wheels would hardly move. "I cannot. I cannot. I cannot," was all he said. The situation looked hopeless. Eventually, however, a little blue engine came merrily puffing along. She was small and inexperienced (she had never been on the other side of the mountain). But she knew what had to be done. She took into her cars the toys and food, and said to herself, "I think I can. I think I can. I think I can." And she did it—up, up the steep incline, and down, down with gathering speed, until she reached the city in the valley. The little engine smiled and seemed to say as she puffed on her way, "I thought I could. I thought I could. I thought I could. . . ."[1]

Jennifer and I no longer read that story, but its "moral" is an important part of a culture that has shaped us. *The Little Engine That Could* taps an American myth flowing like a subterranean river deep in our national soul. Anything—anything at all—is possible for those who work hard enough and have a "can do" spirit. The most famous stories on this theme, of course, were those of the nineteenth century author, Horatio Alger. He wrote over a hundred books for boys that were filled with heroes who inevitably rose from "rags to riches" by dint of perspiration and persistence.

In this land of opportunity go-getters *get* provided they have enough *go*. There may be difficulties, but those who stay in the race win the trophy; when the going gets tough, as they say in the locker room, the tough get going. This tune is so familiar it bounces off our eardrums like muzak in the supermarket—hardly noticed, simply part of the background. We all know why the goodies made it to the boys and girls on the other side of the mountain: at least one little engine had the guts, the red-blooded, stars-and-stripes-forever, can-do spirit to say, "I think I can." I didn't read my daughter just another story; I baptized her into the American Jordan.

Just try raising kids without solemnly intoning during at least a dozen dinners a year that they can achieve anything they desire with enough faith and hard work.

Johnny has been moping around the house for the last three days, looking as if he had scratched his Suzuki or was in terror of new zits before the Big Date or some such tragedy, and you finally have had enough of the door slamming and his yelling at his sister and grunting through dinner, and you say, "All right, out with it. What's bugging you?" After twenty minutes of grilling, he finally reveals the Problem: he knows for a fact that all meaning in life will be lost if he doesn't make linebacker in the football tryouts.

So that's it. Fortunately, you're prepared. It has nothing to do with sex; you can handle this one. You've learned your lessons in the school of positive thinking. Everything in your experience, from Miss Interminable's Sunday-school lessons to the half-time harangues you endured when State was kicking the stuffing out of you in the play-offs, to your recent rise from a second-floor closet to the twenty-ninth floor office with a view, has prepared you for this moment.

"Son," you begin, like one who knows the chapter and verse by heart, "go for it. You can do anything you want if you want it badly enough. The guys who make it in this world are not the flash-in-the-pan dazzlers but the dedicated ones, the guys who keep trying against all odds, the guys who keep tackling the dummy when the others have gone to the showers. You know what I mean? Never mind that you weigh a hundred and twenty pounds. Diamonds are small but hard rocks, boy, hardest things on earth . . ." At this point you're a bit worried that maybe you've just dated yourself. By now they've no doubt discovered something harder, and Johnny's sure to have heard about it in science class; you're just hoping it won't undercut the truth of what you're saying, the truth which is as comfortable as slippers in the wardrobe of your beliefs—it might be a little worn here and there, but so what? Who would ever think of replacing it?

Think positively. This maxim is our real national anthem. And its theme is repeated in countless slogans which prod us along the road to a fulfilled tomorrow: Every cloud has its silver lining. . . . Look on the sunny side of life for a brighter day. . . . You can if you think you can. . . . Inch by inch anything's a cinch. . . . Every problem hides a possibility . . . and so on. These are capsulized forms of our common·wisdom. We live in "an officially optimistic society."[2]

Just as the flowers in my yard don't grow by themselves but need cultivation (water, fertilizer, weeding), neither does optimism bloom without certain factors contributing to its growth. What has cultivated the American can-do spirit?

**Positive Thinking Helps**
The first factor fostering optimism is that a positive spirit often provides the inner energy needed to clear the hurdles of life. Everyday experience proves why the slogans of optimism have become so much a part of our proverbial wisdom. My body rolls out of bed more easily when I anticipate a productive day; my marriage works considerably better when I choose to congratulate my wife on the portion of the toast that is *not* burned; my children will develop healthier self-images if I affirm them rather than nag them. We've all experienced this. In general, positive thinking works.

A few months ago my wife and I decided our youngest daughter was not getting enough exercise. So I resolved to do something about it.

"Joy," I said one evening at dinner, "how would you like to start running with me?"

"Yuk."

"I want you to think about this. Wouldn't it be fun going for a little run with Dad? We could talk. It would be special." I was already imagining the advantages: some quality one-on-one time with a child who often missed her usually-at-a-meeting daddy. It would even be a good example to my parishioners. Who knows, I might even become an illustration in somebody's book on effective parenting. I was getting excited about this.

Joy wasn't. "It wouldn't be special for me," she mumbled.

"I have an idea. Let's work hard, and in two months we'll enter the Del Mar family fun run!"

"But Dad, I'm only eight." (It sounded like, "But Dayaaad, I'm only aayaat!")

"It's only a mile, a family fun run. We could all be together—Mom, Jennifer . . ."

"It wouldn't be a *fun* run for me."

I was not about to be discouraged. After all, I'm a communicator. I make my living motivating people. I know my daughter.

"All right, Joy, here's what I'll do: if you run one mile without stopping, I'll give you twenty bucks."

I had her. But she had set her heels too firmly on this matter simply to give in, though I suspected she wanted to. I was whistling her tune and we both knew it. What happened next was as close to victory as I would get that evening: silence. She was thinking.

Not another word passed between us on the subject for about a month. Then came her announcement. "I have something to say," she declared, with a tone of voice signaling something momentous. "I have decided to run a mile. Tonight." I nearly choked. She might just as well have announced her intention to climb Mt. Rainier.

"Well . . . uh . . . that's interesting," I stammered, not sure what to say. For as certainly as I wanted her to exercise, I just as certainly didn't want her to fail. (Those parental instincts of protection are strong!) "Don't you think you ought to wait until the morning when you're feeling fresh?"

"Nope."

"You can't run on a full stomach, you know."

"I can."

What was I to do? She was determined. That day she had seen a toy she couldn't live without, and she needed twenty dollars to get it. I tried to help her understand that a mile was a long way for an eight-year-old to run. But my caution couldn't penetrate her closed mind. "Dad, I *can* do it," was all she said.

So I measured a mile with my car odometer, asked for the hundred and twelfth time if she was sure she wanted to try it, and then put on my running shoes to keep her company. Not that she needed it. She wasn't in the mood for fellowship: her brow wrinkled with hard concentration, her lower lip thrust defiantly forward and her neck stretched toward her goal. We were off with no time for small talk.

And like the little engine pulling her load over the mountain, she did it. I was proud of her: she had done the difficult thing—with a can-do spirit. I hope she never forgets that experience, for like all of us she will need that same determination to meet life's challenges. Positive thinking often helps with running the race set before us.

### A City upon a Hill

The second factor fostering optimism has to do with our heritage. Presumably, positive thinking works as well for people in other countries as it does for us. Why, then, are we the "officially optimistic society"? Why is the practical power of the can-do spirit, for us, a national myth? Why is it a significant part of our cultural ethos, as American as apple pie and Fourth of July fireworks? The reason can be summarized in one word: destiny.

A sense of destiny gave birth to America. Our Pilgrim fathers and mothers felt the providential hand of God upon them guiding them into an important future. John Winthrop, for example, while sailing across the Atlantic in 1630 with the future leaders of the Massachusetts Bay Colony, preached a sermon to his fellow passengers aboard the *Arbella,* striking the keynote of American history: "We shall be as a City upon a Hill, the eyes of all people are upon us."[3] Those who laid the cornerstone of our republic believed they were fulfilling a mission: their destiny was to be that city upon a hill which would beam its light to the nations, witnessing to the blessings of God and the life of faith.

> Never was a people more sure that it was on the right track. "That which is our greatest comfort, and meanes of defence above all others," Francis Higginson wrote in the earliest days in *New-Englands Plantation,* "is, that we have here the true Religion and holy Ordinances of Almightie God taught amongst us . . . thus we doubt not but God will be with us, and if God be with us, who can be against us?"[4]

By the Revolutionary era a century and half later, the bright colors of this theological interpretation of colonial destiny had faded. A broader pluralism had replaced the narrow exclusivism of the Puritan founders; if we were still "under God," it was so in only the most general sense, in a sense which would encompass the Calvinist Jonathan Edwards, the Deist Thomas Jefferson, and the thousands for whom separation from European traditions also meant separation from things religious. Though the biblical heart of this positive spirit may have stopped beating, the sentiment lived on. The can-do spirit continued with no necessary connection with the Holy Spirit.

And thinking positively provided energy for the taming of two frontiers: building institutions and conquering the land. To establish governments, schools, churches, businesses and eventually industries, requires hope, a necessary belief in the future, a feeling that one's labor will make a difference. So the can-do spirit became oxygen in our national blood, providing energy for work that needed doing.

The land, too, would not yield to exploration, settlement and cultivation without that optimism we call "the frontier spirit." It's probably impossible to overestimate the influence western lands have had on our national psyche. From the time when "wilderness" meant western New York, to the adventures of the Oregon Trail, to the entrepreneurial enclaves of California suburbs, there has always been something beyond the horizon providing another chance to succeed. What limits could there be for a nation commissioned by God and seemingly in possession of a vast continent of abundant resources? Historians refer to the sentiment extant during the westward expansion as "manifest destiny," that sense that we were destined, manifestly so, to take hold of this land. And it carries over into the sunbelt expansion of our time. There's opportunity out west, or so many believe. Thus roots continue to be dug up from eastern and midwestern soil to be transplanted in southern California communities like mine, where we call anyone who's been here ten years or more an "old timer."

When President John Kennedy challenged the country to create a new future, he spoke of the "New Frontier." With this phrase he drew upon a deep emotional heritage. On the frontiers of life anything is possible—even going to the moon; what really matters are not fancy degrees and aristocratic titles and material privilege, but callouses on the hands and steel in the will and goodwill in the soul.

We are a young nation, of course, and such feelings are perhaps appropriate for youth. As nations go, we're still in adolescence. A teen-ager might anguish over her looks and relationships, and be nearly hysterical with insecurities, but at least she has a future about which to dream. The right boy will come along, someday her figure will fill out, college will be more fun, her own car will make all the difference —these things are the stuff of her fantasies and entirely natural for her age. In the same way, a young nation imagines possibilities yet unrealized. There is some evidence that we are feeling older now, not as nimble in spirit. But if so, it's a recent development; we're hardly ready for the convalescent home.

Our institutions, compared with those of other countries, are barely out of the crib. While doing graduate work in Scotland I preached one Sunday in the Dalmeny Kirk. I was asked to announce that the following Sunday the congregation would be celebrating its eight hundred and fiftieth anniversary—in the same building! My church recently marked its fortieth anniversary. It's not surprising that the two churches have very different levels of energy and enthusiasm.

Our nation emerged with a sense of destiny. That confidence found ample opportunity to express itself in a land of vast opportunity. Every frontier meant a chance to begin again, a possibility waiting to be seized. When you add to this the energy of youthful hope, you can understand why we are "an officially optimistic society."

**Technological Idolatry**
The third factor fostering optimism is our trust in technology. Where there is a will, the saying goes, there is a way. And this slogan has been elevated to confessional status by our nearly idolatrous dependence on scientific experts who can make all things possible with microchip omnipotence.

This, too, is a part of our heritage. Consider Benjamin Franklin (1706-1790), who has been called "the quintessential American."[5] His well-known *Autobiography* tells the archetypal story of a poor boy who made good through hard work and clever application of his knowledge. Born into the home of a candle maker, he was unable to afford a college education. But he tutored himself, and with discipline went on to achieve so much that Thomas Jefferson called him "the greatest man and ornament of the age and country in which he lived."[6] His work as minister to France did much to help win the Revolutionary War, and many historians consider him the finest diplomat America ever sent abroad. His contribution as a civic leader was equally impressive: he set up the first subscription library in America, organized the first hospital and founded an academy which later became the University of Pennsylvania. And he gave to us, through his writing, many of the sayings that have shaped our language of positive thinking: "Early to bed and early to rise, makes a man healthy, wealthy, and wise." "God helps them that help themselves." "Lost time is never found again." "Little strokes fell great oaks." Benjamin Franklin incarnated, as it were, the can-do spirit; he personally embodied our national myth.

But what picture comes to mind first when you think of Franklin? I'll bet it's this: a man standing in a storm, wearing a three-cornered hat and knickers, flying a kite with a key resting on the wire close to his hands. Yes, we know the story well: lightning struck the kite, traveled down the wire, caused sparks to burst from the key, and this proved that lightning is electricity. Franklin's invention of the lightning rod followed. He also invented bifocal lenses, through which you may be reading these words, and the fuel-efficient stove which today bears his name. Benjamin Franklin, poor boy who made good, was a *practical* man. This one who accomplished so much in political and civic endeavors set his can-do energy to work on scientific problems and instead of getting lost in theoretical speculations made good use of his knowledge, discovering useful inventions. This, too, is why he was "the quintessential American."

In Franklin, positive thinking and science became one flesh, and the marriage survived better than most in our day. The belief that anything is possible with enough determination and perseverance finds an agreeable bedfellow in the technological revolution.

Technology has indeed opened doors that only a generation ago seemed forever shut. A woman in my congregation recently celebrated her one hundredth birthday. As we sang "Happy Birthday" to her, I thought of all the changes she has lived through: from riding horses to flying at supersonic speeds; from wire telegraphing to satellite telephoning; from telling stories about the man in the moon to watching a man on the moon; from dreading measles to having (as in her case) an artificial hip installed. Now if science can do all this, why shouldn't we believe in the possibility of all things?

"Man is the measure of all things," said Protagoras in 450 B.C. But with the development of the scientific method, the measure of all things became the measurer of all things, and eventually the master of all things. For millennia, humans had lived in awe of the natural universe around them, impotent before its mysteries and power. But with modernity came measurement; the universe moved to the far end of a telescope or microscope. And knowledge confers power; it takes only a short step to move from measuring to mastering, from studying to controlling. Do the toys need to get to the boys and girls on the other side of the mountain? With our computers we can surely find a way, and with our present technological skill we can build whatever it takes. "I think I can" is now replaced by the technologically assured "Of course I can."

Well, even if *I* can't, *someone* can. Enter the Expert. As our technological powers increase, so also does our dependence on those with specialized skills. Until a few months ago I wrote with a fountain pen. If it ran out of ink, I filled it. But recently I joined the twentieth century, and now I'm writing on a computer. If it breaks down, I won't even attempt to fix it. Without so much as a worried pause, I will take these steps: (1) Call my secretary to see if she can fix it; if not, I will (2) call a church member who dances around computers all day; if that person gets stuck, I will, of course (3) call in an Expert. I might be irritated at the delay but certainly not paralyzed by fear. If they can make these things, they can surely fix them. Someone, somewhere, will know the answer to my problem.

The technological revolution and the Experts it demands have kept us moving nicely down the road of positive thinking. Do you have a problem? Never fear. If Experts can get a person on the moon, they can certainly get on top of your problem.

### The Newest Frontier: Personal Fulfillment

Personal experience, a sense of destiny, vast frontiers of opportunity, the technological revolution, problem-solving Experts—these factors have helped create a generally unquestioned faith in the power of positive thinking. But in the last two decades a significant shift has taken place. The frontier has moved.

Our sense of national destiny is not as clear as it once was; many of us are not as certain that God's blessing rests on all we do. In the sixties and seventies we looked in the mirror, and what we saw on our national face was a scowl of racial hatred, eyes of shame over a questionable war and a blemish of political scandal we could not hide. Certain names still create difficult emotions for some of us: Selma, Vietnam, Watergate. . . . The face in the mirror has grown older; wrinkles witness to a lost innocence. Youthful optimism doesn't come as readily.

And the frontiers, geographical and technological, are rapidly vanishing. Except for some sunbelt suburbs, the wilderness is pretty well tamed by now, and technology, while still accessible to the

Experts, has advanced in complexity beyond most of us.

With the diminution of these external factors, which have traditionally nourished the positive spirit, there has emerged a new frontier. We couldn't all migrate to Alaska, so what were we to do? We had the growing affluence and leisure to discover a whole new universe: ourselves. The frontier moved inward. Concurrent with the social traumas of the sixties and seventies, the human potential movement sent us into a self-improvement orgy of psychological therapy and sensitivity groups, fat farms and sex camps, Eastern meditation and self-esteem seminars, jogging and rolfing, bean sprouts and megavitamins, and so on—journeying further and further into a new and improved *me*. Whereas our forebears walked through forests and ended the day in a circle of wagon trains, today we walk across hot coals to build our confidence and cool our feet in a hot-tub circle of interpersonal sharing.

Tom Wolfe labeled the seventies "the Me Decade" and described this national seizure of self-centeredness in religious terms:

> Whatever the Third Great Awakening amounts to, for better or for worse, will have to do with this unprecedented post-World War II American luxury; the luxury enjoyed by so many millions of middling folk, of dwelling upon the self. . . . Where the Third Great Awakening will lead—who can presume to say? One only knows that the great religious waves have a momentum all their own. Neither arguments nor policies nor acts of the legislature have been any match for them in the past. And this one has the mightiest, holiest roll of all, the beat that goes . . . *Me* . . . *Me* . . . *Me* . . . *Me*. . . .[7]

The Experts are still with us. Only now, instead of wearing the lab coats of technicians, they wear the running shorts of the sports therapist or the gold necklace of the chic hypnotist or the flowing robes of an Eastern guru; the "culture of narcissism"[8] needs its Experts every bit as much as the culture of computers.

While recently calling on a parishioner in the hospital, I was astonished to see visiting her not only a doctor but also a psychiatrist, a psychologist, her daughter's psychologist, another pastor, a youth director—and then me. Perhaps she was unusually well-attended by us Experts, but she was only relatively further down the road that our whole society seems to be traveling.

Our local newspaper reported that the latest convenience, for those in the know and with the means, is to have a physical fitness counselor come to your home for private instruction in tummy firming and backside curtailment. No longer does one need to mess with sweaty locker rooms; just pick up the telephone and call Rent-a-Jock. Don't risk ruining yourself with ordinary calisthenics; you might bulge and curve out of place, and what then? Well, then you would have missed your chance for a more perfect body. So call that Expert! You already rely on them for mental health, spiritual growth, financial counseling, legal advice, relational problems and leaky plumbing. The frontier of the Perfect You is waiting to be explored and tamed, but don't forget the lessons of technology: you need an Expert, and then indeed anything is possible.

## Discussion Questions

1. A dominant theme in American tradition tells us that we do not need to live with unfulfillment. How does this affect our view of the Christian life? of prayer?

2. In what ways were you taught to believe in positive thinking and in the can-do mentality? When has positive thinking "worked" in your life? When hasn't it?

3. How would you define the American dream? How is it different than Christian hope? How do your goals for the future fit within these two perspectives?

4. Whether at home, work, church or wherever else, in what ways do you use Experts? How do you think a dependence on Experts affects the way we approach problems? How do you think it affects the way we relate to God?

# CHAPTER THREE

# Can-Do
# Faith

*C*hristian *faith reflects the milieu in which it lives. Just as a child* cannot grow without being influenced by his or her environment, our faith cannot live without being shaped by the culture surrounding it.

We might imagine that our faith escapes this, that it preserves the water of biblical truth in crystalline purity, free from society's sediment. But such is never the case. This does not mean our understanding of the gospel remains forever imprisoned by our environment; surely God's Word can break through to criticize and reshape our assumptions. But for that to happen we must recognize the assumptions that *are* there.

The cultural atmosphere of positive thinking affects the under-standing and expression of Christian faith for many; in some groups, the can-do spirit may be nearly as important, in practice, as the Holy Spirit.

The most recent goal of positive thinking, personal fulfillment, seems to correspond with certain aspects of biblical faith. Jesus promised an abundant life. What more could we ask? So we threw open the doors of the sanctuary to the human potential movement (the quest for a maximized *me*) and warmly extended to it the right hand of fellowship.

And the Experts also have taken their places in the pew. They are publishing books, distributing videos, offering seminars and making almost as many promises as miles they've traveled. By the grace of God and the help of an Expert, your little engine can get to the other side of the mountain.

But positive thinking is not the same thing as Christian faith; it falls way short. For starters, it doesn't leave room for the concept of sin.

**The Broken Circle**
What is sin? It's more a description of who we are than what we do. Of course the Bible does forbid sins, specific actions contrary to God's will, but the problem runs deeper than that. When the apostle says that "all have sinned" (Rom 3:23), he didn't mean simply that we all need to tidy up our lives a bit here and there; he meant that we are sinful—full of sin—because sin has become the dominant structure of our lives.

Once upon a time, the story begins, God created heaven and earth, plants and animals, and at the summit of his creation he made in his own image man and woman. Whatever else it may mean, being made in God's image at least tells us that we have a will—an ability to choose and create and risk—and with this gift comes the capacity to build or destroy relationships with others.

The first humans used this power in a destructive way. Adam and Eve were given a whole garden in which only one tree was off-limits: the tree of the knowledge of good and evil. This was the one thing they couldn't have, but being parents of the humanity we know so well, it was the one thing they decided they couldn't live without. As it happened, they couldn't live with it, but the tempter didn't mention that possibility. The serpent enticed them to eat by telling them, "You will not die. For God knows that when you eat of it your eyes will be opened, and you will be like God, knowing good and evil" (Gen 3:4-5). *You will be like God.* Here we have the heart of the matter. Sin expresses itself in concrete acts of disobedience (Adam and Eve did what they weren't supposed to do, and thus turned their backs on God's will), but fundamentally it is an act of rebellion in which the sinner tries to take God's place.

"Well, whew!" someone might say, "I'm safe. The last thing I want is to be God. I mean, I have no hankering to run the universe. I have enough trouble just keeping my own ducks in a row."

But think about it. God's place is the center place, in control of things. I'm a sinner because that's where I want to be—not necessarily directing galaxies and governing nations, but at the center of *my* world. I want things to go my way; I work to make that happen, and I react badly when it doesn't. When I break God's commands, it's because I want something that in his wisdom he knows I shouldn't have. When I'm petty, filled with ugly emotions, it's because my will has not prevailed. Jealousy, for example, gnaws at my insides when someone gets something I want.

Explaining sin metaphorically, Donald Baillie tells us to picture

God inviting his children to join in a great circle for the playing of his game. In that circle we ought all to be standing, linked hand in hand, facing toward God at the center, with that central Light illumining the faces of our brothers and sisters as we dance together with the rhythm of love universal. But instead, we have turned our backs on God and the human family. We no longer face the Light, and in this position we can neither hold hands nor even see the faces at the circumference. Each of us intently plays his or her own little selfish game; each wants to be the center, and there is blind confusion.

Because we were created for community we are not happy in this situation. The Light of God still shines; only now it casts its beams on our backs. In front of us, shadows create a strange and unfriendly world. We might try to make ourselves happy, dancing ever more furiously, but the shadows dance still more mockingly, and things are worse than ever. We might even attempt to make ourselves good, but that too fails. For as we try to increase our happiness and improve ourselves, we remain focused on ourselves, and this self-centeredness is the very thing from which we need to be saved.[1]

The circle has been broken. Moreover, that brokenness has, as it were, penetrated us. Our hearts tell us things are not right. We want something different; we need something different. But if we stay at the center and in control, the problem intensifies. We might *think* we know the medicine we need, but as long as we rely on our own prescriptions, we're like cancer patients trying to cure ourselves with more cancer.

### Pious Sin

The most subtle and, therefore, dangerous form of sin is the sort that says its prayers and goes to church. A person may be very religious yet retain the essential structure of a sinful life. Self-centeredness may adopt a religious vocabulary and express itself in praiseworthy desires, but it remains self-centeredness. At Halloween a child can wear angel wings or a devil tail, but she is the same candy-loving kid underneath. In the same way, sin wears a variety of masks, and it's important to recognize this if we wish to escape deception. Sin disguises itself most effectively with piety.

For this reason, I am uncomfortable with the common evangelical practice of inviting people "to accept Jesus" or "to invite Jesus into your life." As long as I invite Jesus into my life, I can maintain my essential self-centeredness. Jesus may be an important part of my life, adding a wonderful new dimension, but I'm still in control. The gospel of Jesus Christ summons us to something far more radical: it seeks to save us from ourselves, to convert us, to turn us toward God so that he can take his rightful place at the center of our lives.

Without that conversion God is only a means to other ends, a utilitarian god whom we keep on hand to satisfy our wants. All around us we see evidence that this perversion pervades contemporary Christianity. James Gustafson has recently noted that

religious belief, trust, and practice, are offered as useful instruments for getting on well in the business of living, for resolving those dilemmas that tear individuals and communities apart, and for sustaining moral causes, whether they be to the right, the left, or in the middle. Both individual pieties and social pieties become instrumental not to gratitude to God, the honor of God, or service of God, but to sustaining purposes to which the deity is incidental, if not something of an incumbrance.[2]

### Sweating, Straining Spirituality
Having turned away from God and having become centered in

ourselves, we feel empty inside. And at this point of longing we are most vulnerable to being influenced by the culture we live in. The American dream tells us we *can* find fulfillment if we think positively and work diligently. And Experts, of course, will always be around to provide necessary assistance.

But what happens when our legitimate longing for wholeness looks to the can-do spirit as its savior? We end up treating God as if he were little more than a utilitarian Expert. Nothing essentially changes in our situation. Pagan sin may have been traded in for spiritual sin, but the sin remains, the structure of life which keeps the *I* firmly in control.

Let me offer two examples. First, consider the "name it and claim it" gospelers of instant gratification. As children of the King, they contend, we have a right to live like princes and princesses. God has a storehouse of bounty and waits for us to claim what is ours. "God's will is prosperity."[3] So! Do you "need" a higher paying job? a new Mercedes Benz? a more exciting sex life? a successful remake by the beautician? Well, name your pleasure and claim your treasure. All you need is enough faith. If the heavenly payments seem slow, not to worry; just pray more earnestly and believe more fervently. You have a right to God's goodies; so if delivery lags, well then, you have obviously done something wrong. It must be disguised sin. Or debilitated faith. Or deficient praying. The secret for success: try harder.

The second example I offer is the well-meaning but often unbalanced emphasis some groups place on divine healing. Certainly much of Jesus' ministry, according to the New Testament, involved physical healings; so also did that of the apostles. And the Bible seems to promise us the same sort of power (see Jas 5:14-16). So, we might ask, why did I then recently bury a young mother of three whose body was eaten away by cancer?

A few weeks before she died I received a telephone call from a person who confidently claimed that we would witness a modern-day miracle if enough faithful prayer was offered. I was afraid of what he might say to the poor woman, and my fears were well-founded. A few days later he heaped a pile of guilt on her that, for the moment at least, caused more pain than the disease. She wondered what she had done wrong. Did she have unconfessed sin? Did she lack faith? Did she pray incorrectly? When I stood by her bedside she released a torrent of fear: "Pastor, teach me how to pray." And I knew what she wanted. She wanted to be given the magic formula, the perfect combination of words that would have unlocked heaven's medicine chest and brought healing.

What went wrong? She believed in the power of prayer; I believed; most of the church believed. But in the end she died just as the doctors said she would.

Some would say we didn't believe enough or even that I had failed her. According to their belief system, if I had had the proper faith and training in spiritual warfare I could have pulled it off. God would have wiped out those malevolent cells and dispatched her from the hospital.

So what is wrong with these gospels of prosperity and healing?

Both are close to the truth, close enough to be dangerously seductive. But at center stage in each example stands the believer, with floodlights focused on the effectiveness of his or her faith in the midst of difficulties. Both promise transcendence over life's limits—*provided enough human effort is expended.*

Certainly other examples could have been given. Religion like this comes dressed in a wide assortment of vestments: the liberal Protestants who struggle for justice to prove their "goodness"; the Roman

Catholic who out of fear never misses a Mass; the possibility thinker who dishonestly admits no doubts or difficulties for fear of losing God's blessing. These efforts are often performed with the hope that if enough of the right things are done, God will respond.

The cultural air we breathe fills us with self-confidence. So many voices assure us that we owe it to ourselves to strive for personal fulfillment that we feel that God must want this for us too. Thus we transpose the popular music of positive thinking into a religious key. We speak of the need for stronger faith, more discipline and so forth. But the tune remains the same. You can get to the other side of the mountain if your spirit sweats and strains—especially if you bring in God as the ultimate Expert. God is there to help you get what you need. If you're still grinding slowly up the mount of desire with no sight of the summit, you obviously need to work harder at getting God's attention. Fortunately, he has many deputy-Experts writing books and offering seminars to show "how to." Just don't lose hope. Remember: you can if you think you can.

Perhaps I have been creating a caricature; few explicitly preach this sort of message. But the cumulative effect of our intense hunger for more and the subtle accommodation of the biblical witness to the surrounding cultural influences leads us to a situation not far from the picture I've sketched. There are many discouraged Christians to prove it. For when we let ourselves ride after windmills in a dream world of positive thinking and self-struggle, keeping the *I* firmly in the saddle, we eventually wake up in the hard light of reality.

### Discussion Questions

1. What is the "abundant life" Christ promises us? How does it differ from our culture's view of personal fulfillment?

2. Inviting people to "accept Jesus" or "to invite Jesus into their lives" subtly

encourages them to keep ultimate control of their lives. What are some other ways we use our faith to keep God from controlling the center of our lives?

3. What are some things you desire that God doesn't want you to have? Why do you desire them? Why does God not want you to have them?

4. Have you ever thought that if you said the right words (for example, praying "in Jesus' name") or performed the right act (for example, claiming a promise) that God would respond in a given way? What do you think about such methods? If you think such methods can be legitimate, what qualifications would you put on their use?

# AWAKE

The main emotion of the adult American
who has had all the advantages of
wealth, education, and culture
is disappointment.
*JOHN CHEEVER*

# CHAPTER FOUR

# Confessing
# the
# Limits

I *have often sat with couples on the verge of committing matrimony and* have just as often wondered whether my pastoral guidance was being heard above the voices of optimistic anticipation singing in their hearts.

The young woman has long dreamed of marriage, and though the man next to her may not be Mr. Perfection, he's pretty great—great enough to help her build a happy life. But what will happen when she discovers his difficult side and starts feeling less important to him than his work? What will happen when, in spite of a loving family and a nice home, she feels an intense loneliness welling up from the deep recesses of her being?

Her fiancé, too, has had his dreams. Now he has fallen in love, and *fallen* aptly describes it. He has tripped over his passion and happily plunged into a swift current of emotion, the undertow pulling him beyond all reasonable caution. But what will happen when, a few years later, he looks at the woman next to him in bed and sees that clearly she isn't a Playmate of the Month? What will happen when at midlife something within him erupts like a volcano, spewing out feelings of longing and depression?

What will happen when the couple in front of me scrape their noses against the brick wall of reality?

### Personal Disappointment

Let's state it as clearly as possible: not every dream comes true. Eventually the most positive thinker wakes up to this fact. Perhaps a little engine in a children's story happily chugs her way over the mountain by saying, "I think I can," but in real life some mountains are too high and the going too tough.

Popular wisdom tells us to focus on the half-full part of the cup rather than on the half-empty part. As I pointed out in the last chapter, experience proves that a positive outlook often provides the inner energy needed to meet life's challenges. But an important truth often gets sacrificed on the altar of optimism by the priests of positive thinking: while the cup may be half-full, it is *also* half-empty. Spiritual maturity requires that we learn to drink from this half-empty cup.

Feelings of unfulfillment vary in intensity and pain. The dieter who misses chocolate ice cream, for example, suffers differently than the widow who misses her husband. Nevertheless, I think we can distinguish between two broad categories of personal suffering caused by the half-empty cup: that which results when we feel incomplete in some way (as in failing to get the hoped-for promotion) and that which comes when we suffer the painful blows of life (as in having terminal cancer).

Psychologist Abraham Maslow, in *Motivation and Personality,* theorized that in the hierarchy of human needs, "self-actualization" is the necessary final step for full development of the personality. "A musician must make music," Maslow wrote, "an artist must paint, a poet must write, if he is to be ultimately at peace with himself. What a man *can* be, he *must* be. He must be true to his own nature."[1]

Maslow correctly perceived the restless need for fulfillment that stirs within us and propels us to different levels of achievement. But does anyone ever *feel* totally fulfilled? I doubt it. I have certainly never met a person who experienced unambiguous peace, a sense that she has become all she was meant to be. And apart from our Lord, it's hard to think of historical figures whose dying words were, "It is accomplished!"

Alexander the Great conquered Persia but broke down and wept because his troops were too exhausted to push on to India. Hugo Grotius, the father of modern international law, said at the last, "I have accomplished nothing worthwhile in my life." John Quincy Adams, sixth President of the United States—not a Lincoln, perhaps, but a decent leader—wrote in his diary: "My life has been spent in vain and idle aspirations, and in ceaseless rejected prayers that something would be the result of my existence beneficial to my species." Robert Louis Stevenson wrote words that continue to delight and enrich our lives, and yet what did he pen for his epitaph? "Here lies one who meant well, who tried a little, and failed much." Cecil Rhodes opened up Africa and established an empire, but what were his dying words? "So little done, so much to do."

So much for the high achievers, we might think. But what about us normal folks? It's no different. What's normal is living with a sense of incompleteness, the feeling that we have unfinished business at the center of our lives.

A few years ago my daughter Joy asked me to take her fishing. Somehow the idea got into her head that this would be fun. My experience has proved this a wrongheaded notion, and so, I'm sorry to say, I procrastinated, hoping she would forget the idea.

Then we visited my sister and brother-in-law on Thetis Island (a little emerald gem set in the Canadian San Juans), and there was no escaping the inevitable. When Joy's Uncle Kenny announced a fishing expedition, she bounced off the walls of the little beach house, wired with 220 volts of excitement. For years she had relentlessly begged to go fishing, and now her dream was coming true.

On the appointed morning Uncle Kenny and I got into the boat with two little girls, three little boys and untold numbers of little herrings. Picture the scene: two fathers and five kids under the age of twelve. You can imagine what it was like. Lines tangled under the boat, fingers cut by line, eyes nearly gouged out with flying hooks—everything I had expected, and more.

But for a few minutes it seemed like it would all be worth it. Joy had a bite. A big one, fighting. From the enthusiastic chaos of cousins in the boat you'd have thought Moby Dick had just been harpooned. Amidst shouts of encouragement and general confusion, Joy strained to reel in her catch, her little arms doing their tired best to hold on to the sharply arched pole. It was all I could do not to take over for her, but this was her adventure, the fulfillment of her dream.

My nephew Aaron spotted the fish first, and from his whooping I knew it was big as we had guessed. Uncle Kenny managed to net the monster—one of the biggest, ugliest rock cod I had ever seen. Rocky, however, wasn't finished with the fight. He jumped around the boat in a mad frenzy while we tried to beat him into submission. Finally, we won; he, as it were, passed on.

As cries of victory went up from our boat I noticed Joy—with no joy. She sat in a corner of the boat, by herself, close to tears. Fishing was not what she had imagined. Her prize lay on the deck—a scaly, bloody mess, with a face only a mother cod could love—and she wanted nothing to do with it. When her grandmother tried to take a picture, the fishergirl wouldn't get within an arm's length of her catch. The next morning, as we were all enjoying fried fillets, Joy decided she wasn't hungry.

Haven't you experienced feelings like that? You wanted something so badly, but when you finally got it you descended into the emotional pits. Perhaps it was an advanced degree, or a new relationship, or a baby, or a promotion—anything, really—and with a can-do spirit and hard work and the grace of God you achieved your goal. Then what? Well, life goes on, and in the going on of life you still felt incomplete. Some years ago Peggy Lee recorded a hit song titled, "Is That All There Is?" Most of us have probably asked that question.

And some destinations are never reached. Even the most positive thinker would have to admit that not all his or her desires have been achieved. There are limits in life; some mountains are too steep even to lay track, let alone to chug our way over the summit. No, it's not just the high achievers who live with unfulfillment. We all do.

Even spiritually mature Christians. But shouldn't they, at least, be exempt from this problem? They possess the promise of an abundant life; the Spirit of God dwells in their hearts. Christians may sometimes feel discontent, granted, but isn't this because they have let slide the disciplines of discipleship? Don't they simply need to pump up their pooped-out piety?

No less a Christian than the apostle Paul had to learn to live with the brokenness of human life. In the middle of his great theological affirmation of the love of God in Christ Jesus our Lord, he recognized "the sufferings of this present time" (Rom 8:18). He was not thinking about minor irritations, but sufferings—deep hurts, unrelieved pains. As Paul saw it, everything was affected by it. "The whole creation has been groaning as in the pains of childbirth right up to the present time" (8:22 NIV).

### Faithful Suffering

The pain Paul had in mind was much more than unrealized dreams of health, wealth, and blissful happiness; it was the distress of sin, which, like a disease, invades our life, weakens it and marks it for death. In such a world suffering often happens to us: babies are born with defects, children get leukemia, friends are killed by drunk drivers, spouses leave for more interesting partners—the list could go on and on. In uncountable ways, life hurts.

After conducting a memorial service for a friend who had died of cancer, I went home to a daughter whose hands were cracked and bleeding from eczema. As I tucked her into bed she said, "Daddy, we've asked Jesus to heal me. Why doesn't he? Why should little girls have to hurt like this?" Good question. If Jesus is in charge, as we affirm in our confession of his lordship, why should cancer or eczema or countless other problems assail Christians as well as nonbelievers?

Being a Christian—trusting the God revealed in Jesus Christ—does not exempt us from life's hurts. Yet many assume that their spirituality must be terribly amiss if they suffer, and this unnecessary guilt often intensifies pain. We bring some problems upon ourselves, to be sure, because of weakness or even blatant disobedience. But undeserved suffering also comes our way—suffering sometimes outrageous in its injustice.

According to Scripture certain kinds of suffering happen *because* we are Christians. Paul, explaining the "advantages" of being an apostle, told the Christians in Corinth about some of the troubles he had seen:

Five times I have received at the hands of the Jews the forty lashes less one. Three times I have been beaten with rods; once I was stoned. Three times I have been shipwrecked; a night and a day I have been adrift at sea; on frequent journeys, in danger from rivers, danger from robbers, danger from my own people, danger from Gentiles, danger in the city, danger in the wilderness, danger at sea, danger from false brethren; in toil and hardship, through many a sleepless night, in hunger and thirst, often without food, in cold and exposure. And, apart from other things, there is the daily pressure upon me of my anxiety for all the churches. (2 Cor 11:24-28)

About the only thing that hadn't yet happened to him was being trampled by a herd of wild elephants.

Where was his faith? Sustaining him, certainly, and getting him through the tough times. But his faith—robust as it must have been—didn't shield him from difficulties. He stuck with God, but that meant he got pretty wet himself when it was God's will to wade into the waters of affliction.

Paul's list of trials didn't embarrass him. Just the opposite! He seemed to view suffering as a sort of badge of authentic discipleship, rather like the football player who, though in pain, proudly points to his wounds as proof that he had been in the thick of it.

He was a follower of *Jesus,* after all, and Jesus didn't exactly keep to the rose-strewn path. Jesus kept the faith, was perfectly obedient to the Father—and ended up on a Roman cross.

Jesus suffered. Paul suffered. We all endure suffering at one time or another. It emerges from inside our longing hearts when unfinished business leaves us feeling incomplete. It assaults from without though we've done our best to trust God. It may even strike *because* we live obediently in a disobedient world.

## The Wider World of Suffering

Personal suffering usually first wakens us to the limitations of life. Some, however, have this feeling intensified by being aware of the wider world of suffering. Just watching the evening news should mortally wound some cherished assumptions, especially our faith in the power of positive thinking. What sense would it make to exhort listless Ethiopians, weakened by drought-caused malnutrition, to develop a can-do spirit? It's an absurd, cruel thought. *The Little Engine That Could* must make about as much sense to someone dwelling in a Calcutta slum as do the Upanishads to us.

Dominique Lapierre has written a fine book about a Calcutta slum called Anand Nagar, which translated means the City of Joy. Less than three times the size of a football field, this wretched parcel of land contained 70,000 people.

It had the densest concentration of humanity of this planet, two hundred thousand people per square mile. It was a place where there was not even one tree for three thousand inhabitants, without a single flower, a butterfly, or a bird, apart from vultures and crows—it was a place where children did not even know what a bush, a forest, or a pond was, where the air was so ladened with carbon dioxide and sulphur that pollution killed at least one member in every family; a place where men and beasts baked in a furnace for the eight months of summer until the monsoon transformed their alleyways and shacks into lakes of mud and excrement; a place where leprosy, tuberculosis, dysentery and all the malnutrition diseases, until recently, reduced the average life expectancy to one of the lowest in the world; a place where eighty-five hundred cows and buffalo tied up to dung heaps provided milk infected with germs. Above all, however, the City of Joy was a place where the most extreme economic poverty ran rife. Nine out of ten of its inhabitants did not have a single rupee per day with which to buy half a pound of rice. Furthermore, like all other slums, the City of Joy was generally ignored by other citizens of Calcutta, except in case of crime or strike. Considered a dangerous neighborhood with a terrible reputation, the haunt of Untouchables, pariahs, social rejects, it was a world apart, living apart from the world.[2]

As I read Lapierre's story of men and women whose cups were not even half-full but contained only a few drops, I wondered how many of our aspirations would survive in such an environment. Most wouldn't; they would shrivel into trivial insignificance. If all our energies went into fighting off death, there would be no time left to dream about, let alone work for, many of the things we think so important. Admonitions to think positively would be as relevant as teaching the art of igloo construction in the Sahara Desert. Some mountains are too steep for little engines—even those with good heads of can-do steam; there are Himalayan ranges of suffering which form insurmountable barriers to human fulfillment.

## Waking to Depression

Waking from a pleasant dream is difficult. Harsh beams of reality can easily make us want to roll over to recapture the dream. It never works, though; the new day must be faced. Or to change the image, one who has had to face the realities of unfulfillment might try to deny them by running harder and faster down the road to success, straining with a more fervent determination. At some point in the race, however, a heaving heart and weakening legs cause an exhausted collapse.

Then what? The result is often depression or despair. Depression occurs with an inner loss, with the loss of part of one's self. Despair occurs with an outer loss, with the loss of part of one's world. Depression destroys concern ("I just don't care anymore"), and despair destroys hope ("the world is going to hell in a handbasket"). A subtle difference, perhaps, but a difference nonetheless.

There are different types of depression—from a normal grief reaction resulting from a loss, to endogenous depression due to a chemical imbalance in the body. Most of us, however, suffer the depression associated with grief over losing something. Negative events obviously trigger depression: death of a spouse, deteriorating health, loss of employment, financial reverses and so on. But positive events, too, can send us into the pits. Hoped-for things, such as marriage or childbirth or vocational advancement, often cause slumping spirits. Why? Because a serious loss takes place—the loss of dreams. In gaining certain goals we lose the planning and striving which become familiar parts of our lives.

Cliff Harris, safety for the Dallas Cowboys, described his feelings about winning the Super Bowl: "You have something to look forward to only if you do lose. After one that we won, I looked over at Charlie Waters and whispered, 'But whom do we play next?' When you win the Super Bowl—I hesitate to say it—you're depressed."[3]

When we awake to the realities of unfulfillment, either by achieving or failing to achieve certain goals, the result may be depression. It would be wonderful if our faith insulated us from this problem; unfortunately, it doesn't. Many preachers and writers would lead us to believe otherwise, but they need to read their Bibles more carefully.

Consider the prophet Elijah. After achieving some incredible spiritual victories—he correctly prophesied a three-year drought, raised a widow's son from death, was miraculously fed by ravens at the brook Cherith and, in a sort of spiritual Super Bowl, walloped 950 pagan prophets with the result that the nation turned anew to God—he ended up pouting under a broom tree in dismal depression. "I have been very jealous for the LORD, the God of hosts," he whined, "for the people of Israel have forsaken thy covenant, thrown down thy altars, and slain thy prophets with the sword; and I, even I only, am left; and they seek my life, to take it away" (1 Kings 19:10).

It wasn't true. God had a faithful remnant of 7000. But depression distorts perspective.

What did God do in response? Throw him out of the fellowship of faithful prophets? Give up on him? Not at all. He spoke to him *in the midst of his depression,* not in dramatic ways (wind, earthquake or fire) but in the harder-to-hear still, small voice, the whisper which can barely be heard above cries of pain in the human heart.

Do you suppose the apostle Paul remembered Elijah when he descended into his valley? He told the Corinthians about a difficult time in his life: "For we do not want you to be ignorant, brethren, of the affliction we experienced in Asia; for we were so utterly, unbearably crushed that we despaired of life itself. Why, we felt that we had received the sentence of death" (2 Cor 1:8-9).

Yes, even Christians get depressed. Martin Luther, the great Protestant reformer, suffered periods of black gloom. Charles Spurgeon, regarded by many as the most effective preacher of his generation, was immobilized for weeks at a time by depression and anxiety. Søren Kierkegaard, prolific nineteenth-century author whose thinking significantly influenced modern theology, "suffered all his life with what he termed his melancholy, a condition that today would doubtless be described as that of chronic depression."[4] J. B. Phillips sank into a debilitating depression after the popular success of his paraphrase of the New Testament.

Life is difficult—even for those with faith in God.

### Waking to Despair

Another common response to the harsher realities of life is despair, depression's first cousin. In depression one's heart seems to drop out; there is an inner emptiness, a loss of emotional energy. But in despair one's future seems to drop off the horizon; there is an outer emptiness, a loss of hope.

Despair sometimes comes with personal feelings of unfulfillment. No matter how hard we try, we can't seem to find that elusive fulfillment. So what's the use? The inner energy may still be there, but any effort seems pointless.

Despair can also come when we wake up to the state of the world around us. How can hope exist in a world with countries like Ethiopia and cities like Calcutta? How can hope exist in a world where in our century alone millions have been killed in combat, exterminated in gas chambers and tortured in prisons; millions more have been victimized by preventable starvation and disease? But who has time to worry much about the past when today the two superpowers have amassed the nuclear equivalent of thirty thousand pounds of TNT for every man, woman and child, and humanity seems to be evolving straight into a mushroom cloud?

Yes, our technological power continues to expand, and the desire to believe all things are possible, all problems conquerable and all dreams achievable makes us cling—perhaps desperately so—to that power. But do we really feel any more in control of our destiny? Jacques Ellul described our situation well: "Never have there been so many openings, scientific breakthroughs by the most stupefying, lightening-like extensions of technology. . . . Yet never has man felt so closed in, so confined, so impotent."[5] The very knowledge which makes possible the radiation of cancer cells, for example, makes possible the radiation of earth in an atomic holocaust.

Clarence Darrow, after a distinguished public career, sent back advice to the younger generation coming after him: "If I were a young man, with life ahead of me, I think I'd chuck it all, the way things are now. The odds are too great against you, and anyway, the world is all wrong nowadays. I certainly have no encouragement for the youngbloods just starting out looking for jobs. The sooner they jump out the window, the sooner they'll find peace."[6] So speaks the voice of despair.

And yet, and yet. The hunger remains. Perhaps we have lost hope; perhaps the future seems bleak. But we *do* want more. Why would we have such longings if there is no hope for fulfillment? Are we merely out of step with reality?

Malcolm Muggeridge, in his autobiography, tells of a scene he has often imagined, both sleeping and waking:

I am standing in the wings of a theatre waiting for my cue to go on stage. As I stand there I can hear the play proceeding, and suddenly it dawns on me that the lines I have learnt are not in this play at all, but belong to a quite different one. Panic seizes me; I wonder frenziedly what I should do. Then I get my cue. Stumbling, falling over the unfamiliar scenery, I make my way on to the stage, and there look for guidance to the prompter, whose head I can just see rising out of the floor-boards. Alas, he only signals helplessly to me, and I realise that of course his script is different from mine. I begin to speak my lines, but they are incomprehensible to the other actors and abhorrent to the audience, who begin to hiss and shout: "Get off the stage!" "Let the play go on!" "You're interrupting!" I am paralysed and can think of nothing to do but to go on standing there and speaking my lines that don't fit. The only lines I know.[7]

The play seems to be about life in a world of limits and suffering, and yet the lines you know *by heart* are about fulfillment and joy. You seem to be in the wrong place at the wrong time, hungering for a meal you'll never eat, and when you let yourself think about it you feel as if the hot coal of despair has dropped into the pit of your stomach.

The desire to escape depression and despair becomes fertile ground for the seeds of idolatry. *If God hasn't spared us the pains of unfulfillment, perhaps another god will.* There are always three at hand, ready to lend assistance to weary travelers along the never-ending road to happiness.

### Discussion Questions

1. In what ways do we ignore or repress the "half-empty" part of life?
2. Undeserved suffering visits everybody. How do you respond to this statement?
3. Have you ever wanted something with your whole being and worked hard to get it, but it never worked out? How did you feel? How do you feel about it now?
4. Have you ever had one of your dreams come true only to be disappointed? Why did you feel this way? How do you feel about it now?
5. Have you ever been depressed or in despair? How did it feel to experience these things? How did you stop feeling that way? What do you think is the difference between depression and despair?
6. Should Christians ever feel depressed or be in despair? Why or why not?

# CHAPTER FIVE

# False
# Gods:
# Materialism,
# Power &
# Religion

**W**hen we wake from the American dream and find ourselves unable
to deny certain limits in life, we naturally want relief. Depression or
despair, or even simple sorrow, cry out for it. There must be a way,
we think, to get around the limits, to escape our difficult circumstances. At this point we are especially vulnerable to three temptations which promise the rest and ease we think we want. Materialism, power and religion readily present themselves to us with letters
of recommendation from the surrounding culture. They are false
gods, but nonetheless attractive and powerful.

## Materialism

Not long ago I visited Christians in East Germany, and the experience challenged me in unexpected ways. One evening I had a rather heated political discussion with a pastor who shepherds a congregation trying to live with faith and courage in an antagonistic environment. Unlike most of his fellow citizens, he had been able to visit the United States for an extended period as an official guest of one of our churches. He said, with considerable passion, "You Americans like to talk about freedom and high-sounding ideals. But you should be more honest. What you really value is the power to satisfy your material wants."

I defended "the American way" with an unnecessary intensity belying my nagging suspicion that he was correct. For when I thought about it later I had to admit that what I would miss most in that Communist country would not be political freedom. No, what I would find almost unbearable is living in a small apartment, having to wait thirteen years to buy a miserable excuse for a car and not having our almost paralyzing variety of goods from which to choose.

The first god aggressively seeking to claim our loyalty is materialism. Whether we realize it or not, many of us bow in servitude before it; many trust its power to bring fulfillment.

Materialism commands our attention because we *are* material creatures. We need food, shelter and clothing, and we work to provide these things for ourselves and loved ones; the more we have, the more secure we feel.

Not only do we have material needs, we experience many material joys. What would life be like without physical pleasures? A lick of chocolate ice cream, the joy of sex, sinking a hole-in-one, enjoying a beautiful painting (the list is almost endless!)—not that you can't live without these things, for surely they aren't strictly necessary, but without them life would be leaner.

The security and joy materialism brings are so concrete and immediate that materialism tempts us to look to it for salvation. Karl Marx took this to an extreme and built an entire economic, political and historical philosophy on it. Yet many Americans, who would retch at the thought of being labeled "Marxists," differ only in details, having built their lives on the same foundation.

Greed fuels the engines of contemporary Western life. Our national economy seems to depend on an expanding rate of consumption, and given human nature, it has probably bet on a sure thing. And just in case greed's power should slacken, Madison Avenue is there to stoke the fires. According to one study, the average American family is "exposed" to 1,600 advertisements each day.[1]

A belief in an increasing power to consume is part of our national mythology, an implicit part of our destiny. For this reason, we would never elect anyone to public office who did not promise to raise our standard of living, and we listen carefully as the day's "leading economic indicators" are nightly reported with the life-and-death seriousness of a nurse informing a doctor of a patient's vital signs.

Robert Maynard Hutchinson accurately observed that "our real problems are concealed from us by our current remarkable prosperity which results . . . in part from our new way of getting rich, which is to buy things from one another that we do not want, at prices we cannot pay, on terms we cannot meet, because of advertising we do not believe."[2]

Leo Tolstoy told a story about a peasant who was offered all the land he could walk around in one day. The man hurried to get around as much as possible, but his exertion was so great he fell dead just as he got back to where he had begun. He ended with nothing. And that is precisely what material desire produces—nothing. The more you feed it, the more it grows, till only the hunger itself remains. John D. Rockefeller said, "I have made many millions, but they have brought me no happiness." John Jacob Astor left five million, but at the end of his life lamented, "I am the most miserable man on earth." Henry Ford longed for the happier days of doing a mechanic's job, and Andrew Carnegie commented, from personal experience no doubt, "Millionaires seldom smile."

Some of us might think we would like to try that sort of unhappiness. At least wealth enables us to choose a more comfortable misery! Indeed, it has undeniable advantages, and poverty in itself is not a good. But we are more than material. To focus only on this one aspect of our humanity, making it the controlling principle of life, leads into a cul-de-sac of unfulfilled desire.

Jesus, too, was assailed by material hunger. And severely tempted by it.

He emerged from the obscurity of the ordinary when John baptized him in the Jordan River. Jesus identified himself with the people in their need and showed his unreserved commitment to God when he waded deep into the waters of repentance.

Then a strange thing happened. Instead of calling a press conference to get the kingdom movement off to a good start, he "was led by the Spirit for forty days in the wilderness, tempted by the devil." In what has to be one of the greatest understatements ever penned, Luke then said simply, "and when they were ended, he was hungry" (Lk 4:1-2).

What could be more natural for Jesus than to want—desperately desire—to turn stone into bread? Why wouldn't he comply with the devil's request but instead simply say, "It is written, 'Man shall not live by bread alone' " (v. 4)?

Because the tempter was asking for a slight shift in priorities—

so that instead of placing first things first, Jesus would give top billing to something secondary, in itself good perhaps, but not the best.

Not that Jesus would never eat again. Certainly he would—in *God's* time. That was the real issue. Bread is a material need and joy. Yet bread may never take first place, for we do not live by bread alone. Bread alone keeps one very hungry. We need more, much more. And that is why materialism turns out to be an impotent god. Exalted beyond its rightful place, it simply cannot deliver the goods—at least the goods we really need.

**Power**

The second god offering to fulfill our desires is power. If you're trying to pull together life's scattered fragments into a coherent pattern of meaning, power presents an apparently reasonable way to do it. Get control of your world, it would seem, and then surely things will fall into place.

Power attracts powerfully. At various times we have all fought for it. In grade school, while taking a turn as class monitor, we early-on discovered its rewards; in high school we longed for the power of belonging to the right group; when married we fought for control of the relationship (what were so many of those early scuffles about if not control—who will get whose way?); in the workplace we watch and wait for the perks of power—the private office, the corner window, the company car—symbolic rungs on the ladder.

Why are we so attracted to power? It offers the possibility of enhanced self-worth; being on top must surely guarantee you're at least as good as the heap. It promises control in a life often ravaged by uncontrollable events. It breathes hope into personal desires. Perhaps most tempting of all, it whispers "Freedom!" into the ears of captives. Whatever the reasons, it's a fundamental drive of human life.

Even Alexandr Solzhenitsyn, a person who more than most has suffered the abuses of power, confessed how he himself coveted it. As a former officer stationed at a transient prison camp, he longed to be chosen group leader by the administration. Silently he pleaded, "Me, me, pick me!" and then experienced the pain of having to remain one of the nobodies taking orders in the ranks.[3]

The German philosopher Friedrich Nietzsche argued that "the will to power" is *the* basic human drive. He held that we desire, more than anything else, control over our selves and creative mastery, and thus all religious concepts, such as eternal life, merely compensate for failures of power. His ideal was the "superman": "The superman is a magnificent man, such as Caesar Borgia or Napoleon, who develops his personality and employs his creativity without regard for laws, institutions, or other individuals. He is the man who ruthlessly pursues his success without any moral scruples."[4] It's not surprising that Hitler's Nazis adopted Nietzsche as the prophet of their new order in the 1930s.[5]

While many of us might question Nietzsche's one-sided analysis of human character and disagree with his conclusions, we would nevertheless find it difficult to disagree with his premise that the drive for power underlies much of human life. But power, like materialism, can't meet the payments on its promises. It doesn't satisfy the hunger for happiness.

In 1923 some of the world's most powerful men met at the Edgewater Beach Hotel in Chicago. Collectively, they controlled more wealth than was in the entire United States Treasury, and for years the media had held them up as examples of success. Who were they? Charles Schwab, president of the world's largest independent steel company; Arthur Cutten, the greatest wheat speculator of his day; Richard Whitney, president of the New York Stock Exchange; Albert Fall, a member of the President's Cabinet; Jesse Livermore, the greatest bear on Wall Street; Leon Fraser, president of the International Bank of Settlement; Ivar Kruegger, head of the world's largest monopoly. What happened to them? Schwab and Cutten died broke; Whitney spent years in Sing Sing penitentiary; Fall spent years in prison but was released so he could die at home; and the others—Livermore, Fraser and Kruegger—committed suicide.

Power never finds satiety. Every taste of power is like a shark's first bloody bite which explodes into voracious hunger. What Henry Fielding said of money is also true of power: when worshiped as a god, it plagues you like the devil. It demands a continually greater sacrifice of the soul, a holocaust of human character, until all that remain are the flames. As O'Brien tells Winston Smith in George Orwell's *1984*, "Power is not a means; it is an end." So we play the games of power, individually and collectively, and the politicking feeds off its own deadly flesh. The final, absurd result is the stock-piled power of annihilation, the nuclear arsenals which seem to have a life of their own, irrationally growing for the sake of growth.

Jesus, too, was tempted to seize an awesome amount of power. According to Luke, the devil offered him authority over "all the kingdoms of the world" (4:5). Imagine what he could have done with that! He would use power with wisdom and compassion. How could he refuse such an offer for God's sake and the world's? All that was necessary was for him to go along with the way of the world, to accept the way things are done, to play the game without changing the rules. With this sort of realism Jesus could have established a genuine kingdom of good, modeled on the highest sort of ethical insights. Why not settle for the attainable good rather than be killed by the seemingly impossible best? Surely he could have continued to preach and even set up a church based on fine humanitarian insights. Jesus was not asked to renounce his ideals or become an atheist. No, he needed simply to tip his hat to the tempter and discreetly bend his knee in recognition of the way things are in this world.[6]

But Jesus knew where such power leads—to the emptiness of raw power, to more of the same and not to salvation. Simply to speak this world's language in a louder volume would not provide the Word needed to bring coherence to our Babel. So he responded by saying, "It is written, 'You shall worship the Lord your God, and him only shall you serve.' "

Not that he would never rule. Certainly he would—in *God's* way. Power would be his, but not as the world knows it.

### Religion

The third god seeking the throne is religion. Religion is the quest for God, the human effort to transcend life's limits through a relationship with the divine. What better way to find fulfillment in life than one which wears the attractive vestments of high aspiration and noble causes?

It's an attractive temptation. Temptation? How can one be *tempted* by religion? Isn't that a contradiction in terms? Isn't the religious person, by definition, someone who more consistently than most resists temptation? Certainly no self-respecting devil would entice you to pray or attend church or do acts of pious charity!

Don't count on it. Evil does its best work when disguised as a good; it seduces most effectively while singing hymns and smelling of incense. "Satan disguises himself as an angel of light," the apostle Paul warns (2 Cor 11:14). And if Luke's order of the three wilderness temptations means anything, he must want us to understand that the tempter reached his climax not with an obviously wicked suggestion but with an outwardly spiritual proposal.

Taking Jesus to the pinnacle of the Temple in Jerusalem, the highest point of the holiest place in the holy city, the devil said, "If you are the Son of God, throw yourself down from here" (Lk 4:9). This was no ordinary temptation. The devil knew his Bible. "Jesus, *prove* your piety," he was saying in effect, "for doesn't the Good Book say that God will dispatch a squadron of protective angels to keep you from even stubbing your toes?"

The tempter urged what must have been for Jesus the most natural thing in the world: to trust God and demonstrate God's trustworthiness. Jesus wasn't asked to renounce his faith or water down his theology; he wasn't asked to make even minor compromises with evil. He was simply being asked to act according to his deepest beliefs.

Can you imagine the effect it would have had on the people of Jerusalem? Soon he would be preaching that not a single sparrow falls to the ground apart from the Father's watchful eye. What better way to illustrate this than by an act of spiritual derring-do? The reporters would have leapt at such a story. By the next day Jesus would have been the talk of the town, the honored guest at the Mayor's Prayer Breakfast and the next speaker of the Temple's annual Distinguished Preacher Lecture Series. Why should Jesus waste time in a backwater region with backward fisherman? Why not go directly to the center of ecclesiastical power? An act of pious bravery would accomplish it—an act hard enough for normal folks, to be sure, but scarcely a day's work for the Son of God. If the promises of Scripture are true, why not put them to the test?

Jesus knew his Bible, too, and his rebuke was sharp: "It is said,

'You shall not tempt the Lord your God' " (4:12).

What would it have meant for Jesus to throw himself courageously into the shielding arms of God? In an act of spiritual enthusiasm he would have betrayed the cause of God by making it his own cause.[7] Under the appearance of robust faith he would have forced God's hand, demanding acceptance as one who believes so heartily. By attempting to justify himself in this way, he would have turned away from the direction taken at his baptism wherein he identified fully with human sin and God's judgment against it. He would have set himself in the right against God.

But if we were in his place, who would not have given in to this temptation?

For Adamic man reaches his supreme form in religious self-sacrifice as the most perfect kind of self-glorification, in which God is in fact most completely impressed into the service of man, in which He is most completely denied under cover of the most complete acknowledgment of God and one's fellows. Jesus did not do this. He rejected the supreme ecstasy and satisfaction of religion as the supreme form of sin. And in so doing He remained faithful to the baptism of John. . . . He remained in obedience.[8]

The temptation to force God's hand with perfect piety—to bow down before the god of religion—finds ready acceptance in a culture already drunk with the wine of positive thinking. A can-do faith, which huffs and puffs its way toward God's blessings, is the first to jump off pinnacles of the Temple, the first to prove its sincerity, the first to hope to impress God, the first to conscript God into its service.

Paul Brand tells the story of Dustin Graham Gilmore, a fifteen-month-old who first became sick in April of 1978.

At first the child came down with flu-like symptoms. The Gilmores took him to their church and the pastor prayed for him. Members of that church believed that faith alone heals any disease and that to look elsewhere for help—for example, to medical doctors— demonstrates a lack of faith in God. Gilmore and his wife followed the church's advice and simply prayed for their son. Over the next weeks they prayed faithfully as his temperature climbed, prayed when they noticed he no longer responded to sounds, and prayed harder when he went blind.

On the morning of May 15, 1978, the day after their pastor preached an especially rousing sermon about faith, the Gilmores went into their son's room and found his body a blue color, and still. He was dead. Again they prayed, for their church also believed the power of prayer can raise the dead. An autopsy revealed the infant died from a form of meningitis that could have been treated easily.[9]

In this example we see admirable sincerity and understandable longing for God's healing in the life of a loved one—something the Bible itself encourages us to have. We cannot criticize such faith without extreme caution. But a distinction must be made between faith which hopes in God and faith which seeks to manipulate God. In a sense the church was saying, "This is the way we think God should act and we will live accordingly so he will conform to our expectations." So in the name of God they closed their eyes and jumped off the pinnacle, and a little boy needlessly died.

One god allows us to stay comfortably in control; the Other forces us to admit that ultimately we have no control. One falsely promises us security, pledging always to act according to our desires; the Other promises to make his own decisions, being more interested that we trust him than in making our lives secure. The distinction is not always clear. The very subtlety of the problem, however, increases the danger of substituting the religious god for the biblical God.

Jesus, too, faced this temptation. Throwing himself off the pinnacle would have been a supreme work of piety. But he refused the seduction of pseudo-spirituality. Giving in would have meant a complete change in his understanding of God's character. Though the false god of religion might be moved by such acts, his Father would not. Jesus taught that God does not wait for us to climb into the heavens; rather, he passionately reaches toward his creation. He searches the wilderness for sheep dumb enough to get lost; he sweeps the house clean seeking misplaced coins; he runs to embrace his prodigal children who still smell of the pigsty. God initiates reconciliation. Jesus announced not another program for renewal; he proclaimed the good news of God's radical grace. All religion, because it turns things upside down and subverts this grace, must therefore be rejected.

"And when the devil had ended every temptation, he departed from him until an opportune time" (Lk 4:13). One translator renders it, "having exhausted every sort of temptation. . . ."[10] In other words, the devil threw at Jesus the *fundamental* temptations; the high priest of falsehood interceded for the false gods who most powerfully threaten human existence.

We experience other temptations, of course. But they are variations and combinations of the three Jesus faced. Sex, for example, struts its stuff in the hope of winning our ultimate allegiance. And it often achieves success. If Augustine once prayed on the road to sainthood, "Lord, give me chastity, but not yet," what chance do we ordinary folks have against the raging fires within?

Why does sex tempt so powerfully? Because it exquisitely unites the three fundamental temptations, a ménage-à-trois of materialism, power and religion. Sexual intercourse provides physical pleasure, certainly, and though not as basic as other needs (food and sleep), it delights the flesh more intensely. And that's not all: sex is power, the power of intimate knowledge and relational bonding. Materialism and power thus united give birth to religious sensations— ecstasy, a momentary standing outside of oneself, a fleeting transcendence of the limits of life. The joy of sex is one of God's great gifts, but when it becomes a god toward whom we look for personal fulfillment, it oversteps its bounds.

When we seek salvation in gods who promise to fill our half-empty cups, when we give in to the temptations of materialism, power and religion, we find that these gods soon prove impotent, unable to fill our desires. Jesus rejected them, and for good reason.

Human desire creates these gods, and thus they cannot rise above human imagination. What if we need more than we want? What if our brokenness requires a healing larger than our minds can conceive? Then we would need a God who knows us better than we know ourselves, a God who has the transcendent power to save us. We would need the holy God of love revealed in Jesus Christ.

## Discussion Questions

1. "You Americans like to talk about freedom and high-sounding ideals. But you should be more honest. What you really value is the power to satisfy your material wants." Do you agree or disagree with this East German Christian? What evidence can you show to support your view?

2. Try to list all the ways our culture tries to promote materialism. What effect do you think this has on your spiritual life?

3. Why do you think power is such a fundamental temptation? Can Christians have or want power without compromising themselves? Why or why not?

4. What are some examples from your own life or from your Christian community of making religion into a god? What is the difference between having a bold faith in God and making religion a god?

5. In what ways are these false gods similar? Why do you think we are susceptible to these temptations?

6. How did Jesus respond to each of these temptations (Lk 4:1-13)? In what ways can his responses be a model for us?

# LOVED

In the year of Grace, 1654,
On Monday, 23rd of November, Feast of St. Clement,
Pope and Martyr, and of others in the Martyrology,
Vigil of Saint Chrysogonus, martyr and others,
From about half past ten in the evening
until about half past twelve
FIRE
God of Abraham, God of Isaac, God of Jacob
not of the philosophers and scholars.
Certitude. Certitude. Feeling. Joy. Peace.
God of Jesus Christ.
*BLAISE PASCAL*

# CHAPTER SIX

# The
# View
# from the
# Sanctuary

**W**hen we resort to the false gods of materialism, power and religion in an attempt to fill the cup of longing, we err not because we desire too much but because we desire too little. We need more than we want.

We think we know what will secure greater happiness—marriage or divorce, a higher salary or professional recognition, steamier sex or deeper intimacy, a new faith or better spiritual experiences—the list is as long as humans are ingenious in imagining greener grass on the far side of the fence. But we don't realize how hungry we really are. Small potatoes won't satisfy; we need a banquet table only God can spread.

Puny desires create puny gods. Materialism, power and religion can elicit devotion, even sacrifice. Eventually, however, we wake up to the fact that our veneration hasn't sufficiently roused the gods to grant the blessing we seek. So we move on to new gods in pursuit of new desires. Sometimes we get what we want; sometimes we don't. In either case, hunger remains.

Pascal succinctly explained the reason for our hunger: there is a God-shaped vacuum in the human heart. Other things or persons cannot fill the void. But we try. We throw into the emptiness material acquisitions, achievements in power and religious highs, and they rattle around like marbles in a barrel. We can never find enough substitute gods to take the place of God.

And even if we could get close to filling the emptiness—close enough, at least, to keep reasonably happy and distracted from the deeper hurts most of the time—the worst problem would remain. We would still be self-centered. As long as this is our perspective, we will never see what we really need.

Children, in their immaturity, often want things their parents know aren't good for them. A six-year-old might beg and badger his mother for another candy bar, fully convinced that if he doesn't get it at once he won't live long enough to see another cartoon. Why does his mother refuse him? Because she hates him? No, of course not. Precisely because she *loves* him she refuses his immature pleading, mercifully saving him from himself.

Do we ever really grow up? Next to children we might seem mature, even wise. But when we relate to God we often act as toddlers, demanding things that are bad for us while refusing the good.

We need to be saved from ourselves. We need to get off dead center. And that's not just a cliché, for the center, if we position ourselves there, is death for us.

Fortunately, God is able to save us. When we meet him, he proves greater than our puny gods, greater than we imagine; he has the power to displace us and capture for himself the center of our lives. Because he is more than we want, he is just what we need.

### Just What We Need

A few days after Blaise Pascal died in 1662, a servant happened to notice a bulge in the lining of one of his master's coats. Tearing it open he discovered a little piece of parchment paper covered with Pascal's own writing. It was a *testimonium* to a life-changing encounter. For eight years Pascal kept close to himself a record of a two-hour meeting with—FIRE. A God "not of philosophers and scholars," not defined and domesticated by tidy systems of thought, but One incomprehensibly greater, the Holy God of Jesus Christ, burned his way into Pascal's soul.[1]

The author of Hebrews exhorts us to offer God "acceptable worship, with reverence and awe; for our God is a consuming fire" (Heb 12:28-29).

Reverence and awe? We moderns are uncomfortable with mystery. We prefer the empirical certainties of scientific explanations. The witches of the unexplainable have been burned at the stake of our reason. We resemble those described in one of Charles Williams's novels who "liked their religion taken mild—a pious hope, a devout ejaculation, a general sympathetic sense of a kindly universe—but nothing upsetting or bewildering, no agony, no darkness, no uncreated light."[2]

"It put the fear of God in him," we sometimes say, but that's about the only time we link fear and God. We Christian communicators, in an attempt to make everything palatable to our contemporaries, quickly explain that the biblical injunction to "fear God" really doesn't mean what it says. In our eagerness to make known the *approachability* of God we often overlook astonishment over the approachability of *God;* we manage the mystery out of people's lives; we try to blow out the fire.

When we turn God into a back-slapping buddy, awe gives way to a yawn and the good news of the gospel shrinks to boring proportions.

Consider Annie Dillard's reflections on our practice of worship:

The higher Christian churches—where, if anywhere, I belong—come at God with an unwarranted air of professionalism, with authority and pomp, as though they knew what they were doing, as though people in themselves were an appropriate set of creatures to have dealings with God. I often think of the pieces of liturgy as certain words which people have successfully addressed to God without their getting killed. In the high churches they saunter through the liturgy like Mohawks along a strand of scaffolding who have long since forgotten their danger. If God were to blast such a service to bits, the congregation would be, I believe, genuinely shocked.[3]

Perhaps we sense the danger in the deep recesses of our hearts. Perhaps fear clutches us more than we consciously know. If so, the practice of religion may be the chief means of avoiding the object of religion. It is difficult simply to ignore God. But by granting him a little space, a religious corner for example, we can more easily keep him at bay. Cage the lion and you can admire him, even be in awe of him, yet carry on as usual without threat.

Psychologists often wisely tell us we should honestly face our fears, and the fear of God is no exception.

Why would we fear God? For good reason! If God is God, then our efforts at playing God are doomed. His sovereignty yanks the ground out from under our feet and leaves us hanging in the thin air of absolute vulnerability. His power exposes our weakness. His eternity underscores our mortality. How can we not be afraid?

When Abram heard the covenantal promise of God, his face hit the ground. When Moses saw the Lord in a burning bush, he hid in fear. When the children of Israel witnessed a brief, fleeting revelation of God in the mountain storm, they said they had seen enough, thanks, and sent Moses to see the rest by himself. When Isaiah had a vision of God, he cried, "Woe is me! . . . For I am a man of unclean lips. . . . My eyes have seen the King, the LORD of hosts" (Is 6:5). When Peter encountered God's power in Jesus, he fell on his knees, saying, "Depart from me, for I am a sinful man, O Lord" (Lk 5:8). When Saul met the living Christ on the Damascus Road, he was knocked flat.

This is what sends hearts into throats and turns knees to jelly: God is holy.

Holiness, for many, connotes a pursed lips austerity on a campaign to destroy anything fun. The word has about it the smell of incense and old hymnals, the sound of Gregorian chants and haranguing sermons, the sight of vestments and Sunday morning rectitude. These things, however, have more to do with religion than holiness, more to do with human attempts to evoke a sense of the holy than with holiness itself.

What is holiness? The Hebrew root *qodesh* apparently developed from the verb *to divide*.[4] The word *holy* originally had reference to "that *which* is marked off, separated, withdrawn from ordinary use."[5] As one theologian stated it, "the holy could much more aptly be designated the great stranger in the human world, that is, the datum of experience which can never really be co-ordinated into the world."[6]

When we join with the men and women of the Bible in confessing the holiness of God, we mean that we recognize God as wholly other than us, as one who does not evolve out of creation but holds creation in the palm of his hand, as one who does not need us but on whom we depend for every heartbeat and breath; we recognize that all our theological systems are but moons, dim reflections, of a blazing Sun.

Because God is so much more than we want in a god, he's just what we need. The holiness of God might scare the wits out of us, but it's gospel truth, good news, because it means God is big enough to move us off center, big enough to save us from ourselves, big enough to fill the vacuum in our hearts.

**A New Perspective**
My wife once gave me, as a birthday present, a ride in a hot air balloon. On the designated evening our family went to an open field, helped spread the giant limp bladder on the ground, and then watched as the burners breathed into it a feverish, frenzied air. At the pilot's signal I jumped into the bouncing basket, and seconds later my family rapidly shrank beneath me.

Immediately my perspective changed. Distance dwarfed everything that minutes before had seemed so large. As I floated high above my community, I thought of all that went on below—loving and hating, working and playing, giving and lusting, planning and failing, laughing and crying, the things we do with such passionate intensity—and it all seemed smaller, less dramatic.

A newborn eagle's world at first encompasses nothing but a nest.

Then it becomes aware of the branch on which its home rests, and for a time this represents all the "treeness" it can imagine. When finally it starts soaring high above the forest, it presumably sees its tree in relation to other trees and the forest in relation to fields and lakes, and in seeing these things it knows more accurately the truth about its home tree.

We need a larger perspective like this when the pain of unfulfillment fills us with depression or despair, or sends us running after impotent gods for relief. If somehow we could be lifted above the immediacy of our hurts, if somehow we could be delivered from the self-centeredness which distorts our view of reality—then perhaps we could discover a new peace, perhaps we could learn to drink gratefully from the half-full part of the cup without resentment over the half-empty part.

False gods can't help. They lack the power to raise us above our desires, for they are simply creatures of our desires.

But the God of holiness, precisely because he transcends our wants, provides just what we need. He lifts us into a higher, wider place. Held by him, we have a better view of things, a larger picture of reality. His power blows apart narrow perspectives; his consuming fire burns to ashes our self-pity.

If this is so, if the holy God has power to save us from ourselves, the crucial question is this: where do we encounter him?

### The Place of the Song-Dream
In *The Wind in the Willows* Kenneth Grahame captures that sense of terrified awe in the presence of the holy:

> "This is the place of my song-dream, the place the music played to me," whispered the Rat, as if in a trance. "Here, in this holy place, here if anywhere, surely we shall find him!"

> Then suddenly the Mole felt a great Awe fall upon him, an awe
> that turned his muscles to water, bowed his head, and rooted his
> feet to the ground. It was no panic terror—indeed he felt won-
> derfully at peace and happy—but it was an awe that smote and
> held him and, without seeing, he knew it could only mean that
> some august Presence was very, very near.[7]

Where is the place of our song-dream, the place where we encounter that august Presence who can make us feel wonderfully at peace
and happy? The poet of the seventy-third psalm discovered the
place, and perhaps his experience can guide us.

He had two big problems. First, he was in a world of hurt: "my
soul was embittered" (v. 21). We don't know the details, but it's clear
he needed more than two aspirin and a good night's rest. Being in
a world of hurt is difficult; being lost in such a world is almost
unbearable. That was the poet's second problem. The theological
compass by which he navigated had proved unreliable. The answers
he had learned as a boy still fell easily from his lips. In fact he begins
his poem with an accepted maxim: "Truly God is good to the up-
right, to those who are pure in heart." *Truly?* That's what he had
been told. That's what he wanted to believe.

But when he opened his door of orthodoxy to vent some honest
feelings, the winds of doubt nearly blew it off its hinges. His theology didn't square with his experience. "For I was envious of the
arrogant, when I saw the prosperity of the wicked. . . . How can
God know? Is there knowledge in the Most High?" (vv. 3, 11).

He had always thought of himself as one of the good guys, as one
with a pure heart. He said his prayers. He gave alms. He did his
best to obey the law. But how do you explain the guys with black
hats? "They have no pangs; their bodies are sound and sleek. They
are not in trouble as other men are; they are not stricken like other

men" (vv. 4-5). It was as if God were going out of his way to make life as comfortable as possible for them! Things were not supposed to work out this way. Sabbath-school lessons promised something different.

The poet was ready to ask for a refund on his theological investments. "My feet had almost stumbled," he said, "my steps had well nigh slipped" (v. 2). The prosperity of the unrighteous and his own misfortune were like banana peels on which his faith nearly slid into ruin.

It seemed like a hopeless muddle of confusion and despair . . . "until," he said, "I went into the sanctuary of God." *Worship with God's people gave the psalmist a new perspective.* In worship he encountered the God of holiness, and being lifted out of himself, being lifted up, as it were, into the presence of God, he saw things differently.

In the sanctuary, the place of worship, the poet took his eyes off his own hurts and off the wicked who were not hurting, and he focused on God. Everything looked different after that. He saw that he had been self-absorbed, self-protective: "I was stupid and ignorant, I was like a beast toward thee" (v. 22). Nevertheless, God continued to hold him by the hand, as a father clinging to a bad, bawling child. He was held by God's right hand, the hand of power and authority. In this life God would be leading him, and afterward, so much the better, for he would be led into glory (vv. 23-24).

With this assurance his former longings lost their intensity. They did not, surely, disappear completely; he would still have liked to be healed. But the eternal perspective gave him desire for something more important, more satisfying, than health. "There is nothing upon earth," he wrote, "that I desire besides thee" (v. 25).

What moved this poet from despair to hope? One thing: worship.

He looked up from his problems to see something bigger than himself, and he knew that though his body be put six feet under, God wouldn't quit being God. God would be his strength and portion forever.

### Leaving the Shore

Daniel Boorstin once asked Thor Heyerdahl, the man who sailed the Kon Tiki to test the theory that the ancient Egyptians navigated the Atlantic in reed boats, if he felt terribly at risk when he suddenly left sight of land and got out into the open sea. Heyerdahl said not at all: the greatest dangers lay along the shore, with the shoals and rocks. He said he felt a wonderful sense of relief when he sailed into the expansive openness of the ocean.

In worship we leave the shore—the narrow inlets of selfish desires, the shoals of disappointments, the jagged rocks of personal pain—and sail into the vastness of God.

To be sure, this ocean has its own terrors. Annie Dillard, commenting that straw and velvet hats seem like inappropriate dress for worship, wrote, "We should all be wearing crash helmets. Ushers should issue life preservers and signal flares; they should lash us to our pews. For the sleeping god may wake some day and take offense, or the waking god may draw us out to where we can never return."[8]

Yes, God may threaten our false sense of security as we hug the familiar shore; he may lead us out of ourselves into an uncharted, frightening region; he may draw us into a place of no return. He is, after all, a holy God.

But while leaving the shore may be more than we want, it is precisely what we need, the first part of learning to live with unfulfillment.

Worship, simply put, begins with focusing on God. It does not mean searching for spiritual ecstasies or cultivating an optimistic disposition or ignoring disappointments. It means turning from the usual preoccupation with ourselves and giving attention to God. In worship we neither deny personal concerns—our longings and strivings—nor cover them with a veneer of piety; we simply ignore them for the moment and look in a different direction. In worship we make room for God at the center of our lives.

Worship, in the original sense of the word, has to do with ascribing worth. A piece of art may be great whether you recognize it or not, but when you ascribe worth to it by entering the gallery and giving it your attention, you submit to it, allowing it to work its powers over you. The painting draws you out of yourself, broadens your imagination and provides new insights.

In the same way, God is God whether I acknowledge him or not, but when I enter the gallery, as it were, through private prayer or by joining with God's people in the sanctuary of praise, I let God be God *for me.* I submit to him and thus allow him to work his life-changing power over me.

Worship is dangerous. It's like playing with fire. Our cherished images of God and of ourselves get reduced to ashes; our efforts to be in control, to be in God's place, go up in smoke; the false gods to which we've sacrificed so much in order to fill the void are charred into ruin. "Our God is a consuming fire."

But this fire refines. It melts our dross and we are burnished into certitude, joy and peace. For this fire, as Pascal discovered, is the God of Jesus Christ.

### Discussion Questions

1. What have Christians lost when they have lost the "fear of God"? Have you

ever felt this "fear"? Should Christians fear God? Why or why not?

2. What do we mean when we say God is "holy"? Why do we need a holy God?

3. Describe your most memorable worship experience. What did you feel and experience?

4. How can worship help us live with unfulfillment?

# CHAPTER SEVEN

# A Refining
# Fire

In The Lion, the Witch, and the Wardrobe *C. S. Lewis describes the* first time the children hear about Aslan:

"Is—is he a man?" asked Lucy.

"Aslan a man!" said Mr. Beaver sternly. "Certainly not. I tell you he is the King of the wood and the son of the great Emperor-Beyond-the-Sea. Don't you know who is the King of Beasts? Aslan is a lion—*the* Lion, the great Lion."

"Ooh!" said Susan. "I'd thought he was a man. Is he—quite safe? I shall feel rather nervous about meeting a lion."

"That you will, dearie, and no mistake," said Mrs. Beaver; "if there's anyone who can appear before Aslan without their knees knocking, they're either braver than most or else just silly."

"Then he isn't safe?" said Lucy.

"Safe?" said Mr. Beaver; "Don't you hear what Mrs. Beaver tells you? Who said anything about safe? 'Course he isn't safe. But he's good. He's the King, I tell you."[1]

God isn't safe. He's the king, wild with holiness. But he's good.

So the advent angels immediately set about to calm the frightened characters in the Christmas drama. To Zechariah, when told that his long-abandoned hope of a son was about to be fulfilled: "Do not be afraid." To Mary, after Gabriel announced that the Lord was with her: "Do not be afraid." And to shepherds, huddled in blankets out on a rocky Judean hillside, scared witless by the glory of the Lord: "Do not be afraid."

Why not be afraid? Because God is good. "To you is born this day in the City of David a Savior who is Christ the Lord." Do not be afraid, for this glory that (understandably) terrifies you, this power that reveals your powerlessness and disrupts your calm securities—this God—comes as *savior*.

### The Wholly Other Wholly For Us

How do we know what God is like? We do not come to a knowledge of God by reasoning our way into the heavens through clever philosophical abstractions or by imagining what a deity ought to be like in order to provide the supernatural help we need to fulfill our desires. We do not, in other words, begin with ourselves. We look to where he has revealed himself. Our knowledge of God can only be received knowledge, something given to us; otherwise, our God remains precisely that—*our* God, a creation of finite minds.

Where has God revealed himself? The testimony of Scripture and the witness of the church point to a person: Jesus Christ. "In him all the fulness of God was pleased to dwell" (Col 1:19). In the man from Nazareth, in that life stretched thirty-three years between manger and cross, God entered into the messed-up affairs of our world, into the pain of our sinful brokenness, into death itself, for one reason: to be our savior.

Just as children use a magnifying glass to focus the sun's energy to burn through a piece of paper, so the whole being of God focuses itself in a baby named Jesus who became an itinerant preacher and died on a Roman cross.

God's otherness, therefore, reveals itself in mind-boggling uniqueness. His holiness, that which sets him apart from us, is this: he chooses not to keep himself separate but to hold us in love.

Theologians sometimes distinguish between God's holiness and love, the former resulting in judgment and the latter in grace. Luther, for example, makes "constant reference to the fact of conflict in God, the fact that God had to wring from himself the resolve to love."[2] But doesn't this split God into two competing characteristics and cut the heart out of any joyful assurance in the gospel?

This theology errs most seriously in that it fails to account for the New Testament's announcement that in Christ "*all* the fulness of God was pleased to dwell" (Col 1:19). Not some, but *all*. The apostle John, reflecting on this revelation of God in Christ, came to an astonishing but logically necessary conclusion: "God is love" (1 Jn 4:16). He was not saying that God *has* love, along with other attributes such as holiness, but that God *is* love. His essential character, that which sets him apart, is self-giving love. Whereas we turn in upon ourselves in sin, God turns toward us in holiness. God is holy because he loves and loves because he is holy. The Wholly Other is wholly for us.

So this is the consuming fire of holiness: love.

## A Warming Fire

"Of all the worn, smudged, dog's-eared words in our vocabulary," Aldous Huxley wrote, " 'love' is surely the grubbiest, smelliest, slimiest. Bawled from a million pulpits, lasciviously crooned through hundreds of millions of loud-speakers, it has become an outrage to good taste and decent feeling, an obscenity which one hesitates to pronounce. And yet it has to be pronounced, for, after all, love is the last word."

Huxley overstates his case, perhaps, but he has a point. The word *love* surely suffers severe abuse in our language. We use it to express commitment or affection or lust or passing delight; we say "I love you" to a person we would die for, and in the next breath, praising our favorite ice cream, say, "I just love it!"

Perhaps the Roman world had the same problem with their words for love. The New Testament writers, in any event, found a seldom-used word—*agape*—to describe the unique love they encountered in Jesus Christ. It was as if they were saying, "Let's not confuse God's love with our previous notions of love. It's unique. We understand it only by looking at Jesus Christ."

In Christ God shows his love to be other-directed; it sacrifices for the sake of the beloved. That God loves us means he gives himself, at great cost, for our highest good. And because of this it is much more than a sweet sentiment, much more than a heavenly smile and divine pat on the head. God's love, being the fire of holiness, warms and refines.

Our sin has broken fellowship with God. Sin's first characteristic is pride, the self-centered attempt to control our own lives. And in trying to seize the center place we have disobediently turned away from God's will. So our most serious problems, in brief, are pride and disobedience. Through these we have disrupted communion with God and thereby cut ourselves off from the source of life, from Life itself. The final result, therefore, is death—the death of separation from God.

But God's love will not leave us in this condition. To pursue *proud* sinners God humbled himself in Christ Jesus. Whereas we humans have sought God's place, the Son of God took our place. He became Emmanuel, God with us, taking upon himself our broken humanity and bearing the guilt of our sin by entering into the death we deserve. His humility cancels our pride.

And to pursue *disobedient* sinners God sent his Son to obey in our stead. Jesus was not only the Son of God but also the Son of Man; he shared our humanity, being like us in every respect—except without sin. He perfectly surrendered his life to the Father, though eventually that meant a clash with the authorities which sent him to a criminal's death. He did this in our place and therefore represents us before God the Father, offering the full "amen" (yes!) on our behalf. His obedience cancels our disobedience.

To death Jesus went, then, in complete humility and perfect obedience. The cross points to a love which seeks and sacrifices and saves.

The story of Jesus does not end with a crucifixion. What prompted the disciples to tell the story of his death in the first place, igniting the fires of faith and turning a band of fearful deserters into globe-trotting martyrs, was this: God raised Jesus from death. In that act the Father was saying Yes! to the Son and Yes! to us in him. In the Easter miracle God announced the victory of his love—the defeat of sin by grace, the annihilation of death by life.

Here, then, we have no tentative love, no conditional offering, no temporary affection. This has nothing of the fickleness with which we are so familiar in our experience of human love. This love doesn't splutter with a half-hearted flicker; it burns with the white-hot flare of holiness. How it burns! It burns into the icy lovelessness of our lives until, at the center, a melting starts.

### An Affirming Embrace

What does God's love mean for the sense of unfulfillment we experience? Can it offer any help when we wake from the American dream?

Isn't it true that at least part of our restlessness emerges from a desire to prove, to ourselves if to no one else, our own worth? If I move up to a higher income level or get a promotion at work or have an ecstatic religious experience—well, I just might feel better about myself.

We've all had the temporary feelings of satisfaction which come from having attained something of significance. One of the gods (materialism, power or religion) smiled on us, and it felt good, very good—until the benediction faded and we were once again left alone with feelings of inadequacy.

At my commencement the president of the seminary spoke about the history and meaning of the annual preaching prize. And then, to my astonishment, he named me the winner. A second later I looked up at my family seated in the front row of the balcony, and they had a look of pride and joy I will never forget. It was a tremendous affirmation. I felt an increased confidence about my gifts and call to preach, a peace that I was headed in the right direction.

Then came the weekly task of preaching. It went well for the most part. I worked hard at communicating God's Word vividly and concretely, and God seemed to use my efforts to connect anew the dry bones of that congregation and even, I believe, to breathe into them his Spirit. Again, I felt affirmed.

One Monday, about a year after I had been installed, my feelings changed. I was mowing our front lawn. There are some things a preacher shouldn't have to do on Mondays, and mowing the lawn is one of them. But there I was, nonetheless, fighting an endless battle against stubbornly healthy grass.

A car stopped a few feet from me. Looking up, I saw a member of my congregation and waved a friendly "hello." By the manner in which she shot out of the car, like a bullet heading for its target, I could tell she was in no mood for small talk.

She announced that she didn't come to church to hear the sort of garbage I was shoveling out (she didn't really say "garbage" but I can't quote her exactly in a book like this). She felt it was just disgusting. And she wasn't sure she would ever again step foot inside the church.

The last comment, by then, didn't come as bad news. After she finally left, the blades of grass didn't know what hit them. I attacked them with a vengeance theretofore unknown in the history of that manse. I hacked and whacked and shredded until they repented of their insulting existence.

When my anger cooled I was left with doubts. How had I failed? A good preacher, I thought, would have led her down the road of faith without losing her. What should I have done differently? That day I didn't think much about winning the preaching prize. I felt like a loser.

That's the problem with feelings of accomplishment. They are so temporary. You stand straighter and step lighter—for a while. But before long little pins prick your bubble and the old sense of incompleteness returns. Perhaps you notice others who seem to have achieved much more than you. Or perhaps, after congratulating yourself on your fine points, you again become aware of the not-so-fine points you can't seem to overcome. Or perhaps your peace vanishes when the monsters of guilt peer inside your memory. Soon you feel as worthless as ever.

The news of God's love in Jesus Christ burns like sunlight through this depressing fog. *God* loves us: this crowns us with royal worth. We have value—eternal value—not because of natural abilities or achievements, but because the King adopts us and declares us princes and princesses.

We are Aldonzas and God is our Don Quixote.

Aldonza serves drunken camel drivers as a waitress by day and in other ways by night. The Man of La Mancha sees this whore and yet sees something more, something no one else sees, and he says, "My Lady."

She looks at him with incomprehension and exclaims, "Lady?"

"Yes, you are my Lady, and I shall give you a new name. I shall call you Dulcinea."

Later Aldonza suffers the ultimate insult. She is raped. Don Quixote finds her hysterical and disheveled; her blouse has been pulled off and her skirt ripped. He says compassionately, "My Lady, Dulcinea, oh, my Lady, my Lady."

"Don't call me a Lady," she cries. "Oh God, don't call me a Lady. Can't you see me for what I am? I was born in a ditch by a mother who left me there naked and cold—too hungry to cry. I never blamed her. She left me there hoping I'd have the good sense to die. Don't call me Lady. I'm only Aldonza. I'm nothing at all."

As she runs into the night he calls out, "But you are my Lady."

The Man of La Mancha, a knight serving his beloved Lady, seeks his adventure. But at the end he is alone, dying from a broken heart, despised and rejected. To his deathbed comes a Spanish queen with a mantilla of lace. Quietly she kneels beside him and prays. He opens his weak eyes and says, "Who are you?"

"My Lord, don't you remember? You sang a song, don't you remember? 'To dream the impossible dream, to fight the unbeatable foe, to bear the unbearable sorrow, to run where the brave dare not go . . .' My Lord, don't you remember? You gave me a new name, you called me Dulcinea." She stands proudly. "I am your Lady."[3]

We may, like Aldonza, feel worthless and unlovable. But God sees the royalty in us. He dreams the impossible dream about us, he fights the unbeatable foe of our sin, he bears the unbearable sorrow of our guilt, he runs into hell for a heavenly cause, and we are affirmed into new life.

### A Refining Fire

The fire of holiness does more than warm with affirmation. It also refines with judgment. Holy love, busily working to secure our best, has no time to waste on sentimentality. God has a great restoration project under way: he is rebuilding our lives—clearing away broken rubble created by sin, laying a new foundation and erecting girders forged in the furnace of his love.

Howard Hendricks once said, "You can't build a skyscraper on a chicken coop foundation." Have you ever seen beneath a chicken coop? *That's* the stuff that needs to be shoveled out of our lives.

So God's love has a stern side to it; his mercy can be severe. Yes, God loves us as we are. But he loves us too much to leave us that way. The author of Hebrews writes, "God is treating you as sons; for what son is there whom his father does not discipline? If you are left without discipline, in which all have participated, then you are illegitimate children and not sons. . . . He disciplines us for our good, that we may share his holiness" (Heb 12:7, 10).

One evening several years ago, as our family gathered around the dinner table, I asked my daughters, "Did you wash your hands?" "No," Joy answered, "but we put some sweet smelly stuff on them."

God doesn't work that way; he doesn't smother our stink with the sweet smell of sentimentality. He cleanses every pore with an astringent love. His love has this quality because it works toward a goal. We could describe his love as teleological; that is, it moves toward a *telos,* an eventual fulfillment.

My love for my daughters also has this teleological dimension. I have more than good feelings about them. I want what's best for them, and as their father I have the obligation to do all I can to help them grow into mature adults. So while I affirm with praise, I also discipline with punishment. If I gave in to their every whim I would be guilty of helping create self-centered brats, distorted human beings. No, I must deny them and set limits and be firm when they go beyond those boundaries—not out of a lack of love but precisely because of the depth of my love.

In the same way, our heavenly Father wants us to mature into adulthood. He mercifully sets limits and disciplines with disappointments; he holds tightly when we are ready to rush into dangerous traffic after a toy; he says no to things we think we need but will harm us, to things we're not yet ready for; he teaches patience and perspective by leading us according to his time schedule rather than our own.

And God does all this to fulfill the purposes of his love. He has a plan: he orders things so that one day we will be as fully human, as perfectly humble and obedient and filled with his love as Jesus Christ. "We know that in everything God works for good," Paul writes, "with those who love him, who are called according to his purpose. For those whom he foreknew he also predestined to be conformed to the image of his Son, in order that he might be the first-born among many brethren" (Rom 8:29).

"In everything God works for good." This doesn't mean everything in itself is good. Clearly, it isn't. But God uses everything—both good and bad—to arrive at the *telos,* to transform those who love him into the image of Jesus Christ.

Often I am asked by people suffering through a problem, "Pastor, why is God letting this happen to me?" I have to admit I don't know. We cannot peek behind the mysterious veil of God's providence. God keeps his own counsel in many things. We do, however, know this: God is working out his loving purposes, and the story isn't yet finished.

The pains of unfulfillment may be great indeed, but they cannot separate you from the love of God revealed in Jesus Christ. You may feel great emptiness in being single or great frustration in being married, you may not have a position equal to your potential or wages equal to your worth, you may be broken in body or crippled in spirit, you may have desires you can name or longings you cannot name—but none of this alters the fact that God holds you with an eternal love that works relentlessly for your ultimate good.

The apostle Paul, after affirming that in everything God pursues his good purposes, concludes his thought with one of the most stirring passages in Scripture:

If God is for us, who is against us? He who did not spare his own Son but gave him up for us all, will he not also give us all things with him? . . . Who shall separate us from the love of Christ? Shall tribulation, or distress, or persecution, or famine, or nakedness, or peril, or sword? . . . No, in all these things we are more than conquerors through him who loved us. For I am sure that neither death, nor life, nor angels, nor principalities, nor things present, nor things to come, nor powers, nor height, nor depth, nor anything else in all creation, will be able to separate us from the love of God in Christ Jesus our Lord. (Rom 8:31-39)

Only the holy God revealed in Jesus Christ can help us as we face the inevitable limits of life. An encounter with him may at first terrify; he utterly transcends us and therefore threatens our self-centeredness. But precisely for this reason he can draw us out of ourselves so the healing can begin. Therefore we must brave the encounter, we must turn to him, we must worship.

And then comes the biggest surprise of all: we discover that the Wholly Other is wholly for us. What separates him in holiness is his will not to be separate, his commitment to love us. This love he has fully revealed in Jesus Christ. In the crucified and resurrected one we see the heart of God, and know, to use Kierkegaard's phrase, that he has imprisoned himself in his own resolve. He will fulfill his loving purposes for us. Sometimes his love may hurt, but this only confirms the seriousness with which he takes us. We have incomparable worth to him. In everything, in the ups and downs and ins and outs of life, God holds us with a love that will not let us go.

### Discussion Questions

1. C. S. Lewis, talking of God, said that Aslan is *not* a tame Lion. What does it mean that God is not tame? How would God be different if he were?

2. How can God be both holy and love? How do these two qualities work themselves out in the person and life of Jesus Christ?

3. Part of our restlessness emerges from a desire to prove, to ourselves if to no one else, our own worth. Has this proved true in your life? How?

4. How does God's affirmation of us differ from what the gods of materialism, power and religion offer us?

5. Looking back on your life, where can you discern God's refining fire at work?

6. In what areas do you think God has further plans for your life?

# FRIDAY

That glorious Form, that Light unsufferable,
And that Far-beaming blaze of Majesty. . . .
He laid aside; and here with us to be,
Forsook the Courts of everlasting Day,
And chose with us a darksom House of mortal Clay.
*JOHN MILTON*

# CHAPTER EIGHT

# The
# Difference
# Friday
# Makes

**S**omething within tells us things are not right with our Maker; we don't feel entirely comfortable with God. We all have unfriendly memories which ambush us just about the time we've found a bit of inner peace. The cock crows and like Peter we remember: things we've done or not done—the muck at the bottom of the well.

The message of the New Testament is called gospel—good news—because it announces that on the Friday we call Good, Christ took our guilt upon himself and carried it into the vast sea of God's forgetfulness.

When I was a seminary student my wife and I lived in an apartment building which housed some interesting people. One of them was a man named Joe, a professional "bookie" connected with organized crime. Of course we didn't know at first that he was a criminal. He was just a man who sat by the pool every day in a white T-shirt and blue bermuda shorts. But gradually, after many casual conversations, we developed a friendship with him.

One day I was talking with him in his "office," another apartment consisting of a table and two telephones (one for incoming bets and another for immediate contact with his superiors), and he pointed to a full sink of water.

"Do you know why I always keep water in the sink?" he asked.

I had no idea.

"Well, let me show you. See this paper? It's special stuff. I import it from Japan. Watch what happens when I put it in water."

It was incredible, like magic. The whole thing disappeared— totally. There wasn't a soggy piece left.

"I keep my records on this paper," he said. "And now you see why I keep a full sink of water. When the cops break down the door, I simply slide the paper into the water, and all the evidence vanishes."

I was impressed. The genius of it all. I had to remind myself that Joe was a genuine criminal, a public menace, a threat to the social fabric of our nation. But he was such a dedicated master of his craft it was hard not admiring him. (Incidentally, his method worked. The police broke down his door several times while we lived there, and they never had enough evidence to convict him.)

I've long since lost touch with Joe, but I tell this story because God's forgiveness does to our sins what water did to Joe's paper. It's as if all our sins were listed on big sheets of this paper—reams of it for that matter—and in Christ God immersed the records of guilt into the water of forgiveness. The evidence is gone. Totally vanished. Your sins, Joe's, and mine—obliterated through Jesus Christ.

### The End of the Game
God has reconciled us to himself, forgiving all our sin. This was his work from beginning to end. We didn't lift a finger to help; we contributed not a dime to the purchase of our salvation. God did it all: he took the initiative, sacrificed himself and mended the broken relationship. We did nothing but get in the way and make things more difficult.

Therefore, the most important word next to the name of Jesus, the word to shelter us in storms of doubt and hold us amidst the rising river of death, the word which we should hear, really *hear,* and let sink deeply into our lives, is this: *grace.*

But this word is difficult to hear, almost impossible to understand. We have had fleeting experiences with grace—forgiveness from a friend, an unexpected gift, a serendipitous turn of events; these, however, are parentheses in the grammar of living. Almost every-thing else confirms a very different law pounded into us by parents and teachers and coaches and bosses and sometimes even spouses: if you want something of value you have to work for it. The good things in life cost plenty. No pain, no gain. The early bird gets the worm. So get out there before anyone else to scratch and peck your way to happiness.

And to provide strength for weariness and hope for discourage-ment the myth of the power of positive thinking comes to our aid. It's like Gatorade and a whiff of oxygen to those worn out from the competition. It provides assurance that victory is just around the corner.

When victory doesn't come, however, and we find ourselves in a heap on the sidelines, we need a truth which comes not from the culture around us but from the God above us. We need to hear that *the fundamental structure of reality is not based on work but on grace.*

Grace means that in the middle of our struggle the referee blows a whistle and announces the end of the game. We are declared winners and sent to the showers. It's over for all huffing, puffing piety trying to earn God's favor; it's finished for all sweat-soaked straining to secure self-worth; it's the end of all competitive scrambling to get ahead of others in the game. Grace means that God is on our side and thus we are victors regardless of how well we've played the game. We might as well head for the showers and the champagne celebration.

Grace is like a dream I had not long ago. I was walking down the hallway of my high school when it dawned on me that in my next class I would face a final examination in geometry. I froze with fear. I hadn't studied all year; I couldn't tell a theorem from a hypotenuse. The day of judgment had arrived. I could only grope in ignorance, guess in stupidity.

The nightmare approached its horrific climax when Mrs. Haynes entered class the next day and started handing back the corrected tests. Every name was called except mine. The worst, I was sure, saved for the last. She said she had a special announcement about the last test to be returned. Humiliation on top of failure. My fingernails dug into my palms. I would embarrass myself and shame my parents. My life was ruined.

Then came her words: "Students, I'd like you all to congratulate Don. He had the highest mark—a perfect exam." The word *relief* just doesn't quite describe it. I was paralyzed with joy. My life was mercifully saved. I had a future again. I also had Mrs. Haynes smothering me with kisses—a situation from which wakefulness mercifully delivered me.

That's grace—unexpected good news, gospel.

Robert Farrar Capon vividly described the rediscovery in the sixteenth century of this message of grace:

> The Reformation was a time when men went blind, staggering drunk because they had discovered, in the dusty basement of late medievalism, a whole cellarful of fifteen-hundred-year-old, two-hundred proof grace—of bottle after bottle of pure distillate of Scripture, one sip of which would convince anyone that God saves us singlehandedly. The word of the Gospel—after all those centuries of trying to lift yourself into heaven by worrying about the perfection of your bootstraps—suddenly turned out to be a flat announcement that the saved were home free before they started. . . . Grace was to be drunk neat: no water, no ice, and certainly no ginger ale; neither goodness, nor badness, nor the flowers that bloom in the spring of super spirituality could be allowed to enter into the case.[1]

When unfulfillment creates a dry irritation in the back of your throat and the half-empty cup from which you're drinking just isn't quenching the thirst, you need to quaff this grace. "Life can be miserable," Lewis Smedes writes, "horrible beyond enduring, the pits. But the secret of grace is that it can be all right at the center even when it's all wrong on the edges. For at the center where life is open to the Creator and Savior God, we are held, led, loved, cared for and inseparably bound into the future that he has for every child that he claims as his."[2]

## Accepting Acceptance
The holy God of love has claimed us in Jesus Christ. To fulfill the

demands of justice Jesus took our place, and the judgment of God against all human sin fell upon him. He took the place we deserve, the place of absolute abandonment. "My God, my God," he cried, "why hast thou forsaken me?" (Mk 15:34). As Karl Barth put it, the Judge was judged in our place.[3]

Because God graciously wills it, his humanity now represents ours. The perfect offering of obedience that we see in Jesus, from his baptism in the Jordan to his death on Golgotha, is now seen by God as *our* submission to his will. It sounds incredible, to be sure. For we are disobedient creatures, anxiously pursuing self-centered desires and trying to spin the world around the axis of our own wills. But God didn't leave us to ourselves.

He has reconciled us to himself, restoring the relationship which had been broken by our sin. This has all been God's work. We are simply recipients of this gift.

But we must be precisely that—recipients. We do not need to labor at reestablishing a relationship with God by winning his favor in some way. The reconciliation is already an established fact, something freely given to us. We must, however, receive this gift. This receiving the Bible calls *faith*. "For by grace you have been saved through faith" (Eph 2:8). We appropriate God's grace "through faith."

What is faith? First, faith—or belief, to use an equivalent biblical word—is *not* a human work alongside God's work; we do not join hands with God in the work of salvation. Neither is faith something we do to get God's attention and merit his favor. He set his heart upon us before we were born, even before the world was created (Eph 1:4). We have faith because he loves us; he does not love us because we have faith. And neither is faith another law demanding that we gather together enough piety to meet its requirements.

"Christ redeemed us from the curse of the law" (Gal 3:13).

Faith, simply put, is trust.

When my girls were little they would throw themselves into my arms, certain I would catch them. The person of faith has this childlike confidence in the loving Father. Faith says, in effect, "God, on the basis of what you've shown me in Christ, I believe you love me. You have forgiven me. You will hold me and never let me go. Therefore, I trust you with my life."

The New Testament story of the rich young ruler (Mk 10:17-22) illustrates this character of faith. One day a man approached Jesus with a pressing concern: he wanted to know what he could *do* to inherit eternal life.

This man was a doer. He had achieved a position of prominence and wealth, no doubt with a dedicated can-do spirit that would have made him a good American. I imagine he was listed in *Who's Who in Israel* with an impressive biographical notation. And now he was determined to go for the big one, the most important goal in life, the Pearly Gates. He was ready to do what had to be done to get into heaven. You have to like him. He had energy, dedication and a great goal.

Jesus began by mentioning the commandments. The man felt relief. So far, so good. He hadn't been spiritually idle, after all. He had given the law his best shot and was proud to say he hadn't killed anyone or bedded another man's wife or cheated on his taxes or misrepresented a competitor or fleeced a gullible client or neglected his parents; he had followed the rules.

"And Jesus looking upon him loved him." Jesus had compassion for this hard-driving high-achiever, enough to say the hard thing, the thing he needed most to hear to be saved. Saved from what? Saved from himself, from his self-confidence and bondage to his own achievements. "You lack one thing," Jesus said. "Go, sell what you have, and give to the poor, and you will have treasure in heaven; and come, follow me."

Was Jesus giving him a new and more difficult law requiring the final achievement, the toughest work yet to be done before reaching the summit of spiritual perfection?

No, precisely the contrary. The one thing this man lacked was wholehearted trust in God. Jesus was demanding a decision: he was to lay on one side of the scales his standard of living and accomplishments, and on the other side God, and then see which side was heavier. Where did he place his ultimate confidence? In himself or in God? By selling his possessions he would be turning away from his hard-earned achievements and throwing himself fully on the mercy of God.[4]

But he couldn't do it. It's one of the saddest verses in the Bible: "At that saying his countenance fell, and he went away sorrowful; for he had great possessions" (10:22). He didn't have the faith to let go of the securities he had built for himself and find his security in God.

Once when I was in Edinburgh, Scotland, I went for a walk in beautiful Holyrood Park in order to climb to the top of Arthur's Seat and enjoy its spectacular view of the city. On the way I passed under the face of the Salisbury Crags, a vertical wall of rock that would challenge the most experienced climber, and saw a lad in dangerous difficulty. He had attempted to ascend the face of the rock but had gotten stuck and was unable to move up or down.

Apparently someone had gone for help, for just as I approached, the police arrived to assess the situation. It didn't take them long to decide what to do. They circled around to the top of the Crags and threw a rope to the stranded climber. At that moment he was faced with a decision: would he rely on his own abilities or would he trust the rope and the police at the other end? Wisely, he chose the latter. It took a great deal of faith for him to let go of the rock and take hold of the rope. But the police didn't fail him, and within a few minutes he was out of danger.

Many of us find ourselves clinging to a rock, unable to move up or down and paralyzed with fear. We have made it part of the way; we have achieved some things. But we're not at the top yet, and we can't seem to find another foothold that won't crumble under the weight of our expectations. What are we to do?

We must grasp the rope God has thrown us. It was woven in love and is made of the tough fibers of grace and is held by the Lord of the universe. We can trust it.

In the first chapter we saw how Mary Sayers, after years of struggling to prove her piety and having it fail, finally gave up and fell into the hands of God. Those hands did not let go. She was accepted just as she was—guilty, anxiety-ridden, filled with doubt. And she was set free by accepting that acceptance.

That is the best definition of faith I know—accepting our acceptance. Paul Tillich, in a well-known sermon, made the phrase come alive for me:

Grace strikes us when we are in great pain and restlessness. It strikes us when we walk through the dark valley of a meaningless and empty life. . . . It strikes us when, year after year, the longed-for perfection of life does not appear, when the old compulsions reign within us as they have for decades, when despair destroys all joy and courage. Sometimes at that moment a wave of light breaks into our darkness, and it is as though a voice were saying: "You are accepted. *You are accepted,* accepted by that which is greater than you, and the name of which you do not know. Do not ask for the name now; perhaps you will find it later. Do not try to do anything now; perhaps later you will do much. Do not seek for anything; do not perform anything; do not intend anything. *Simply accept the fact that you are accepted!*" If that happens to us we experience grace.[5]

When the pain of unfulfillment burns within us, we need the medication of God's grace. For grace tells us that we are accepted just as we are. We may not be the kind of people we want to be, we may be a long way from our goals, we may have more failures than achievements, we may not be wealthy or powerful or spiritual, we may not even be happy—but we are nonetheless accepted by God, held in his hands. Such is his promise to us in Jesus Christ, a promise we can trust.

And if we are held by God we will be held together; we will not fall apart. We will not drop into meaninglessness and despair. We will survive.

Lewis Smedes, in his book *How Can It Be All Right When Everything Is All Wrong?* tells about when he discovered this. He was in the blackest period of his life.

I had never known such lonely pain, never such fear, never such helplessness, never such despair. I was lost, utterly lost. I felt a life of pious trying going down the drain, a life of half-baked belief in grace exposed as futile. I was sunk. I screamed for help, and none could come. I was making my bed in hell.

I lay down in my spiritual waste. But I did not sink! When I flopped into nothingness I fell into God. The old Hebrew lyricist was right, you can make your bed in hell and find your rest in God's hands. It is not a terrible thing to fall into the hands of the living God. No matter what Jonathan Edwards said. His hands are pierced with nails from Christ's cross; his hands are the strength of his love, the power to hold us and keep us from falling into a hell without God.

I discovered, all by myself, in touch only with my final outpost of feeling, that I could be left, deserted, alone, all my scaffolds knocked down, all the stanchions beneath me pulled away, my buttresses fallen, I could be stripped of human hands, and I could survive. In my deepest heart I survived, stood up, stayed whole, held by nothing at all except the grace of a loving God.

I was in the hands of God.

I could live by grace.[6]

## Discussion Questions

1. How would you explain *grace* to someone who is wholly unfamiliar with Christianity? How does *grace* differ from *luck* or *fate*? When in your life have you had experiences of grace?

2. Faith is accepting our acceptance. How accepted do you feel? What may keep you from feeling God's complete acceptance?

3. What do you think it means to "fall into the hands of God"? Is this something you've done? Is it something you need to do?

# CHAPTER NINE

# Never
# Alone

Elie Wiesel, in his autobiographical account of life in a Nazi concentration camp, tells of a rabbi he knew from a little town in
Poland,

> a bent old man, whose lips were always trembling. He used to
> pray all the time, in the block, in the yard, in the ranks. He would
> recite whole passages of the Talmud from memory, argue with
> himself, ask questions and answer himself. And one day he
> said . . . "It's the end. God is no longer with us."

And, as though he had repented of having spoken such words,
so clipped, so cold, he added in his faint voice:

"I know. One has no right to say things like that. I know. Man is too small, too humble and inconsiderable to seek to understand the mysterious ways of God. But what can I do? I'm not a sage, one of the elect, nor a saint. I'm just an ordinary creature of flesh and blood. I've got eyes, two, and I can see what they are doing here. Where is divine Mercy? Where is God? How can I believe, how could anyone believe, in this Merciful God?"[1]

When things haven't worked out the way you had hoped and the pain of unfulfillment grows like a malignant tumor, you're likely to wonder the same thing. You do your best to get God's attention: you pray and read the Bible and attend church and fuel your faith till it's chugging along like the little engine that could. But he seems so unreachable. Though your knuckles are bloody from knocking, the door of heaven remains shut as tightly as the safe at First National at three o'clock in the morning. You feel so abandoned, so . . . alone.

Standing in the middle of the gym after all the teams have been chosen and wishing you could disappear under the hardwood floor; watching television at home during the senior prom; tossing in the bunk the first night of boot camp; driving home from the airport after dropping off your best friend; looking over a plate of hors d'oeuvres for someone, anyone, to talk with and thinking of an excuse to give your hostess before escaping into the more welcoming loneliness of your empty car; waking up in the middle of the night and feeling the silent darkness creep into every corner of your soul; sitting at a restaurant counter on Christmas Eve while little colored lights flicker around a Budweiser sign—it's as if all this loneliness were pressed together and distilled into a pure loneliness, an unadulterated sense of aloneness so potent you're sure one more drop would leave you stretched unconscious on the floor while the world's party carries on without you.

When God takes his leave you're not simply alone, you're lost in a universe with no meaning.

## A Godforsaken God

In one of his plays Peter Shaffer has a character cry out, "An innocent man tortured to death—thorns driven into his head, nails into his hands, a spear jammed through his ribs. It can mark anyone for life, that kind of thing." So it can. And *who* that innocent man was makes all the difference. The Son of God died, and that means we are marked as God's forgiven children.

Good Friday also means something else, something we need to understand: though at times we may *feel* alone in a universe without God, we are not really alone, not in the absolute sense. The cross means that God himself, paradoxically, entered into our godforsakenness.

That Jesus as a man suffered is not difficult for us to imagine. We all face death, after all, and we're too familiar with history to be shocked by a report of an innocent man's torture. But that Jesus *as God* had "thorns driven into his head, nails into his hands, a spear jammed through his ribs" snaps the spine of imagination with an unbearable load. We can never understand fully the meaning of the fact that on a certain Friday outside the gates of Jerusalem the crucifixion of God took place. But we should learn what we can from this event, for it may help us endure the suffering of our own unfulfillment.

Let's be clear about the specific nature of the suffering of the cross. Jesus' suffering there wasn't primarily physical, terrible though that must have been. The worst suffering, when all heaven and hell broke loose at Calvary, was spiritual. Jesus entered the dark eclipse of God, "the dark night of the soul."

All his life he had believed in the trustworthiness of God. He had lived in the perfect peace of a person who knows he's safe, protected by an all-powerful, loving father. He had taught his followers that God, in his goodness, feeds the birds of the air and clothes the lilies of the fields that they need not worry, for they too will be held by loving hands.

Then those hands let go, and Jesus fell headlong into the abyss. He found himself nailed to a piece of rough timber with wild pain shooting from his head and hands and feet and the wildest of all coming from his heart, and where was God when he really needed him? "My God, my God," he cried, "why hast thou forsaken me?" (Mk 15:34), which roughly translated means, My God, where in the hell are you when I need you? The Apostles' Creed states it starkly: "He descended into hell."

With your eyes fixed on that scene, remember: Jesus was fully God. We must fall back on paradoxical statements to describe what happened. God himself entered into the absence of God; God himself was forsaken by God. Here is eternal death in the absolute sense, a death in the being of God himself.

The implications of this for our own suffering are significant.

**Playing Fair**

The first thing we must say about our pain of unfulfillment, when viewed from the perspective of the cross, is that *God understands*. He knows exactly what we're experiencing, not simply in the sense that because he's God he knows everything, so of course he knows how we feel. His knowledge is more intimate than that. He participated fully in human life. He knows what it is to have a story turn into a tragedy; he knows disappointment and loneliness; he knows

the agony of dying in the prime of his life. In Dorothy Sayer's words,
For whatever reason God chose to make man as he is—limited
and suffering and subject to sorrows and death—He had the
honesty and courage to take His own medicine. Whatever the
game He is playing with His creation, He has kept His own rules
and played fair. He can exact nothing from man that He has not
exacted from Himself. He has Himself gone through the whole
of human experience, from the trivial irritations of family life and
the cramping restrictions of hard work and lack of money to the
worst horrors of pain and humiliation, defeat, despair, and death.
When He was a man, He played the man. He was born in poverty
and died in disgrace and thought it well worthwhile.[2]

When I was in my first pastorate this truth ran over me like a Mack
truck on a downhill grade. A greatly loved elder in our church had
just died of cancer—not an unusual situation for a pastor. This time,
though, it was my wife's and my closest friend who had died. I was
a bruised and bloodied shepherd trying to keep a wounded flock
together. In the midst of my confusion and crying out to a silent
heaven, this truth hit hard enough to knock me off my bed of
bitterness: God knows. My friend had died, and in a way so had
something inside me, but God in Jesus had also gone down in
"death's cold, sullen stream." I couldn't accuse God of being above
it all; I couldn't blame him for not understanding my hurt.

You may have bumped your head hard against the ceiling of life's
limits, you may have caught the fingers of your ambition in the door
of a future which has just slammed shut, you may be tired of pushing blistered and bloody feet down an unending road of hurt, and
worst of all, you may be feeling the throbbing pain of unfulfillment
with every beat of your heart. But you can never say that no one
understands what you're going through. God in Jesus has felt the

wild pain shooting from his head and hands and feet, and the wildest of all coming from his heart.

## A Presence in Absence

We need to go a step further. God not only understands our suffering, *he suffers our suffering*. To say he empathizes would not be adequate, for that might simply mean he has a good imagination. He involves himself more thoroughly. He experiences our pain because he actually participates in the brokenness of this sin-wrecked world. You and I can be sensitized by another's pain, but however genuine the feelings might seem, a protective distance remains. We cannot overcome this distance to enter fully into another's hurt. We can only know intimately what we ourselves live through; space and time limit human experience. But God is not so limited. In the language of theology, he is omnipresent. He can be in more than one place at once, and the cross tells us that he freely chooses to be with us in all places of human suffering—in yours and in mine and even in Joe's, as he sits by the tracks with a bottle of muscatel in his hand and an ache in his heart.

Until recently theologians have been reluctant to speak of the suffering of God,[3] but Jürgen Moltmann offers a contemporary expression of God's suffering that I find persuasive. He argues that God "does not suffer out of deficiency of being, like created beings . . . but he suffers from the love which is the superabundance and overflowing of his being."[4] God chooses to suffer because he so loves this mucked-up world that he sends his Son into the middle of it, not just waist-deep but over-his-head-deep, to bear in himself both the consequences of sin and holy judgment against it.

What we deserve for our sin is God's abandonment; strict justice demands that if we turn our backs on God, he should turn his back on us. The Son of God, on our behalf, entered this dereliction. "My God, my God, why hast thou forsaken me?" Who of us can plumb the depths of tragic meaning in that cry? The Father handing over his Son to hell, the Son abandoned by the Father—a rupture in trinal fellowship, a death in God.

In this event the presence of God invaded the absence of God. In Jesus Christ God left no place untouched—no extremity of suffering or spiritual depression, not even hell itself.

Elie Wiesel, in the book from which I quoted at the start of this chapter, recounts a horrifying story about the hanging of a young boy in front of thousands of spectators:

> For more than half-an-hour he stayed there, struggling between life and death, dying in slow agony under our eyes. And we had to look him full in the face. He was still alive when I passed in front of him. His tongue was red, his eyes were not yet glazed.
>
> Behind me, I heard the same man asking: "Where is God now?"
>
> And I heard a voice within me answer him: "Where is He? Here He is—He is hanging here on this gallows."[5]

Yes. For in Jesus, the beat-up Jew who hung on a Roman torture rack, God entered fully into all the pain of this world. And conversely, he took all pain into his own heart. "God's being is in suffering," says Moltmann, "and all suffering is in God's being itself."[6]

When life hurts God doesn't necessarily provide us with answers. We might think that's what we need, agreeing with Nietzsche when he said, "He who knows the *why* can bear any *how*." But that's not what we need most. Answers seldom comfort. Though they beat us into silence, the pain remains. The most profound reasoning still leaves us alone. Job had three "comforters" who were no comfort at all—despite their rational explanations for his suffering. In the end,

God appeared to Job not with answers but with himself, and Job found the presence of a silent God vastly more comforting than the answers given by those around him.

God has not answered our questions about human suffering. They remain: Why does God allow evil? Why do little babies die? Why do good people suffer and bad people prosper? The questions disrupt our walk through life like mad hornets that won't be waved off. God doesn't get rid of the hornets, but he does come near us in Christ, very near, and takes us by the hand and stays with us on the journey—even though the road may take us through deep valleys of longing and over sharp crags of suffering. Because he does not leave us, because he stays with us even when the going gets rough, we know that somehow we will make it to the end of the journey.

### Meeting God in the Desert

Eberhard Busch has an interesting memory of the great theologian Karl Barth.

> One day I came to Karl Barth and he was very nervous. I saw this and asked him what had happened. Then, as was typical for him, he said, "I had a very awful dream." And Barth had a very great sense for dreams. I asked him, "What have you dreamt?" He said, "I was dreaming that a voice asked me, 'Would you like to see hell?' And I said, 'Oh, I am very interested to see it once.' " Then a window was opened and he saw an immense desert. It was very cold, not hot. In this desert there was only one person sitting, very alone. Barth was depressed to see the loneliness. Then the window was closed and the voice said to him, "And that threatens you." So Barth was very depressed by this dream. Then he said to me, "There are people who say I have forgotten this

region. I have not forgotten. I know about it more than others do. But because I know of this, therefore I must speak about Christ. I cannot speak enough about the gospel of Christ."[7]

Hell, in Barth's dream, was a solitary person in a cold desert—absolute aloneness. This hell threatened Barth, as it does all of us. At times, even now, we feel the chill wind of that desert cut into our hearts, and the loneliness becomes so tangible we have no trouble believing in a hell in the hereafter because it's a hell of a life we're living through in the present.

Because Barth knew of this hell he could not speak enough about Christ. The gospel announces that Christ went deep into the wilderness to be with that solitary person, and by his presence he abolished aloneness, he descended into hell and defeated the desert. As Martin Marty said of Christ, "The crucified victim was the *only* forsaken one, the true derelict. The rest of us die in company, in *his* company. God certified his gift and his act and 'raised him up.' Never again is aloneness to be so stark for others."[8]

Christ has taken the presence of God even into hell, and thus we are led to a startling and comforting conclusion: there is no place, no intensity of longing or extremity of suffering or depth of depression or darkness of doubt that cannot also be for us a meeting place with God. If God has sent his Son into the abyss of hell, we can be assured God won't forsake us in the valleys of life.

Too often we live as though this wasn't the gospel truth. When you find yourself in the pits, beaten down with unfulfillment or other pains, don't you feel the need to get yourself out of the dirt and cleaned up before presenting yourself to the Almighty? I certainly do. It's almost as if a little voice inside me says, "Don, you'd better pull yourself together before you can expect much help from God; you'd better live at least a couple of days without being such a spiritual jackass; you'd better log some time in Bible reading and prayer—*then* perhaps you'll stand a chance of getting God's attention."

That voice might be my guilty conscience or perhaps the devil, but one thing is certain: it lies. The God revealed in Jesus Christ tells us something different. He assures us that no circumstance, however dire, can separate us from his loving presence. We may not feel his presence, but that doesn't alter the truth. He *is* Emmanuel, God with us. With us in faith or in doubt, with us in ecstatic happiness or in desperate longing, with us when we feel as saintly as Mother Teresa or as soiled as the Happy Hooker—with us wherever we find ourselves. We don't have to get ourselves into a different place to meet God. We can meet him wherever we are, even if we find ourselves alone in a very cold desert.

### False Optimism Nailed to the Cross

When Jesus was laid in a Judean tomb, something else was buried with him. The cheery optimism which denies life's harsh limitations also died, and positive thinkers who keep trying to resuscitate this corpse should let the dead rest in peace. If history's most perfect human suffered and died, can anyone reasonably dispute the universality of pain in life? Yes, Jesus was resurrected, but he entered new life through the grave, he triumphed through tragedy.

Jesus died, cut down in the prime of his life. Think about it. Here was one who had a spiritual authority which made the pastors of his day look like first-rate incompetents, one who threw demons out of people like a take-charge umpire throwing rebellious players out of a game, one who healed the sick far more effectively than any graduate of Harvard Medical School, one who lived in perfect communion with God and perfect harmony with his brothers and sisters. Yet this man died "unfulfilled."

He had been at his ministry for only three years. For every person enlightened with truth through his teaching, thousands were left in the dark; for every person delivered from sickness, many more remained blind and crippled and leprous and afflicted in various ways. Imagine what he could have done for the kingdom had he lived another decade or two. It was not to be. He died, a man who left no wife, no children, no bank account, no books written, no professional accomplishments—none of the things we think necessary for a successful life.

The next time you're tempted to believe that all your desires can be met with enough work and prayer and positive thinking, remember Jesus. The next time you're beaten down with discouragement, wondering why you can't seem to accomplish all you'd like, remember Jesus. The best of us had the flame of his life snuffed out before the candle had burned down.

And yet we call the Friday he died *Good*. Why? Because "God was in Christ reconciling the world to himself." Because God was fully present in this man who died too young, forgiving our sin and entering every godforsaken desert of suffering to be with us.

On the cross of Jesus Christ we may start building a solid hope. All shallow optimism has been crucified with Christ, but all hope is not dead. If God can turn the blackest day in history to a good end, if that Friday of all Fridays can be called *Good*, then we must confidently hope that God will work redemptively in the suffering of our lives. Indeed, God has promised us this through the resurrection of Christ from death; even as we share the cross, so also will we share the resurrection. But we are getting ahead of ourselves. We live between Good Friday and Easter Sunday, and to this Saturday life we must now turn.

## Discussion Questions

1. Have you ever felt abandoned by everyone, including God? What precipitated this experience?

2. How does it help to know that God understands our suffering? What situations in your life or in the world around you give importance to this truth?

3. Why is it better to know that God "suffers our suffering" than have answers to why we suffer?

4. What does Jesus' life and death tell us about the Christian positive thinker's view that all our desires can be met if we work, pray and believe hard enough?

5. What is *good* about Good Friday?

# SATURDAY

The world breaks everyone and afterward
many are strong at the broken places.
*ERNEST HEMINGWAY*

# CHAPTER TEN

# The
# Good
# News of
# Brokenness

This book began with a frank recognition that things don't always work out the way we would like. Most of us live with an aching sense of unfulfillment. But we have seen that this desert of longing, far from separating us from God, can be the very place where we meet him. When we do, we discover a love which lifts us above misdirected desires and limited perspectives, a love which accepts us and promises never to leave us. We discover, in other words, the love of God in Jesus Christ.

But life still hurts. Though we may be living this side of Good Friday, trusting the grace of God revealed on that day, we're not yet living in the glory of Easter Sunday. It's as if the doctor has declared the defeat of our disease but has not yet released us from the hospital; our bodies still suffer the effects of sickness, and so for a while we must continue to endure the needles of no-nonsense nurses and the noises of never-ending nights. We live in what theologians call the tension between the already and the not yet: we have already been set free from sin and death, but we have not yet experienced the fulfillment of that victory.

So we continue to suffer on Saturday. But because it comes after Good Friday, it is suffering with a difference. George MacDonald said, "The Son of God suffers unto death, not that men might not suffer, but that their suffering might be like his."[1]

Christ didn't die to deliver us from the harsh realities of life. We don't advance directly from his cross to our crown; we don't leap from Friday to Sunday like Superman clearing a tall building at a single bound. There's a whole day to live through, and it's filled with trouble enough to make us wonder if the morrow will ever come. And yet we survive Saturday because Christ died to take our suffering into himself. For this reason, it is no longer the same. It has been transformed, melted in the fire of holy love and recast in the shape of a cross. Christ makes our suffering like his—purposeful instead of pointless, redemptive instead of destructive, life-giving instead of death-dealing.

The Bible, therefore, doesn't view suffering as a calamity to be avoided but as an opportunity to be prized. "Count it all joy," James wrote, "when you meet various trials, for you know that the testing of your faith produces steadfastness. And let steadfastness have its full effect, that you may be perfect and complete, lacking in nothing" (Jas 1:2-4). *Count it all joy?* Is he serious? It's hard enough surviving our trials without treating them as Grand Prizes in a high-paying sweepstakes. Why should we welcome suffering with a smile? Because, James said, it will be good for you; it will help you become a more complete person.

### From Coal to Diamonds

Human experience shows that suffering can strengthen character. Kites fly highest against the wind, and people often soar to surprising heights when the gales of life blow against them. For example, a woman with no trace of bitterness nurses her husband through years of a crippling disease. Or a young man, with cancer consuming his future, lives out his dwindling days as an inspiration to those around him. We wonder how they do it. We can't imagine ourselves coping as well. Then a problem breaks down the front door of our lives, and we meet the intruder with inner resources we never knew we had.

In the fourth chapter I referred to Dominique Lappierre's book about life in a wretched Calcutta slum called Anand Nagar, the "City of Joy." Perhaps you wondered about that name. What possibly could be joyous about such a place? Not the filth, of course, or the disease or the hunger. But Lappierre discovered something more, something which made him believe the city was well-named; he witnessed a tenacious human spirit struggling to survive against impossible odds. Out of that struggle have emerged communities of love and sacrifice, and from that constant fight against death has come a joyous affirmation of life.

A piece of coal may be useful, but it's not something to treasure. Set a flame to it, and its value vanishes in a wisp of smoke; it has neither endurance nor beauty. No bride would be pleased with a piece of coal set in a ring as a symbol of her groom's love. But subject that coal to intense heat and pressure for a million years, and a transformation takes place. It becomes the hardest, most enduring, most treasured gem of the earth. It becomes a diamond.

The same thing can happen with people. The pressures of life can change the soft carbon of a personality into something more enduring, more beautiful.

The Swiss physician Paul Tournier noted that

there is that extraordinary joy which radiates from many a sufferer from serious infirmity, and which contrasts astonishingly with the moroseness of so many of the healthy people one sees on the bus. What is the explanation? Well, I think that it is because their lives demand permanent courage, a constant expenditure of courage; and since courage belongs to the spiritual economy, the more one spends it, the more one has. It is like a current flowing through them and producing joy, the joy of victory over one's fate. This joy in victory is something we find in all those who accomplish a great exploit—in the climber who reaches the summit of the Eiger via the north face; and in every champion in sports, even if they do collapse in tears of exhaustion at the winning-post. Moreover, in a seriously disabled person it is not the victory of a single day, but of every day. Where does the pleasure in living come from? More from struggling than from possessing.[2]

The highest human achievements often emerge out of this struggle; they are attained not in the absence of problems but in the presence of problems. Plato was hunchbacked. Demosthenes, the greatest orator of the ancient world, stuttered (the first time he tried to make a public speech, he was laughed off the rostrum). Homer was blind. Beethoven produced some of his greatest works while deaf. Sir Walter Scott was paralyzed.

Paul Tournier's stimulus for writing the above-quoted book was an article by Dr. Pierre Rentchnick of Geneva titled "Orphans Lead the World." In it Rentchnick reported an astonishing discovery he made while studying the life-stories of politicians who had had the greatest influence on the course of history: all had been orphans. "Dr. Rentchnick compiled a list of them. It contained almost three hundred of the greatest names in history, from Alexander the Great and Julius Ceasar, through Charles V, Cardinal Richelieu, Louis XIV, Robespierre, George Washington, Napoleon, Queen Victoria, Golda Meir, Hitler, Lenin, Stalin, to Eva Peron, Fidel Castro, and Houphouet-Boigny."[3]

This interesting fact led Tournier to study the relationship between deprivation and creativity. Through further research he compiled a list of high-achievers who had lost one or both parents. It included religious leaders: Moses, Buddha and Muhammad. And philosophers: Confucius, Rousseau, Descartes, Pascal and Jean-Paul Sartre. And artists: Leonardo da Vinci, Bach, Moliere, Racine, Camus, George Sand, Kipling, Edgar Allen Poe, Dante, Alexander Dumas, Tolstoy, Voltaire, Byron, Dostoyevsky and Balzac.[4]

Undoubtedly there are complex psychological factors involved in this linking of childhood loss and significant achievement, but I simply want to underscore the fact that problems often provide the heat and pressure necessary to transform coal into diamonds.

### From Brokenness to Wholeness

If this is true for life in general, it is especially true for the spiritual life in particular. Christian faith rests on the love of God revealed in the crucified and resurrected Christ. God's gracious work for us moves from Good Friday to Easter, from death to life. Authentic Christianity knows nothing of an overpowering triumphalism which either denies the reality of human brokenness or promises instant escape from it; on the contrary, it promises salvation in the midst of suffering, triumph in the midst of tragedy.

We should proceed with caution here. We must be careful not to blur the important distinction between Christ's suffering and our own. Christ died once for all the sins of the world. He completed the work of reconciliation; he doesn't need our bit of suffering to finish the job. The gift has been paid in full. We are saved by God's grace and not by our works.

But in Christ God not only *did* something for us, he *revealed* something to us: he presented a paradigm of ultimate reality. The manner in which he saved the world for all eternity—offering life through death, wholeness through brokenness—provides a window through which we can see how things work in the here and now.

William F. Albright, one of the greatest scholars of the ancient world, made this observation in *From the Stone Age to Christianity:*

Nothing could be farther from the truth than the facile belief that God only manifests Himself in progress, in the improvement of standards of living, in the spread of medicine and the reform of abuses, in the diffusion of organized Christianity. The reaction from this type of theistic meliorism, which a few years ago had almost completely supplanted the faith of Moses, and Elijah, and Jesus among modern Christians, both Protestant and Catholic, is now sweeping multitudes from their religious moorings. Real spiritual progress can only be achieved through catastrophe and suffering, reaching new levels after the profound catharsis which accompanies major upheavals. Every such period of mental and physical agony, while the old is being swept away and the new is still unborn, yields different social patterns and deeper spiritual insights.[5]

Many have observed this pattern in their own personal lives. Malcolm Muggeridge, for example, witnesses to the fact that wholeness comes through brokenness:

Contrary to what might be expected, I look back on experiences that at the time seemed especially desolating and painful with particular satisfaction. Indeed, I can say with complete truthfulness that everything I have learned in my seventy-five years in this world, everything that has truly enhanced and enlightened my existence, has been through affliction and not through happiness, whether pursued or attained. In other words, if it ever were to be possible to eliminate affliction from our earthly existence by means of some drug or other medical mumbo jumbo . . . the result would not be to make life delectable, but to make it too banal and trivial to be endurable. This, of course, is what the Cross signifies. And it is the Cross, more than anything else, that has called me inexorably to Christ.[6]

Neither Albright nor Muggeridge would say that suffering *in itself* is good, but both would agree with James that we must "count it all joy." Why? Because it can be used for a good end. Suffering can be redeemed from evil; it can be baptized into the company of God's servants. "The extreme greatness of Christianity," wrote Simone Weil, "lies in the fact that it does not seek a supernatural remedy for suffering but a supernatural use for it."[7]

The good news of brokenness is that it can lead to wholeness. But how? How does God put to good use the suffering of our unfulfillment? He uses it in at least three ways: he shows us how much we need him; he enters our emptiness; and he transforms us into the image of Christ. To each of these we now turn.

### Hanging by the Neck

During my senior year in high school I worked part-time for Dr.

Frederick Cummings, a veterinarian who taught me a good deal about animals and much more about courage in the presence of suffering. He had had polio and was almost totally paralyzed, but that didn't prevent him from seizing life with joyous enthusiasm. He distinguished himself as a fine doctor of small animals; he coached his church basketball team; he worked for various causes in his community; he was a good husband and father; he maintained a lively faith in God. The pressures of his life had turned him into a beautiful diamond.

After school I would go to his clinic and do everything from clean cages to perform very minor surgery. He was the brains, you could say, and I was the hands. When there was a lull in the work we would talk about God and girls and politics and books—he was interested in everything. Then, at the end of the day, I would help him into a van and take him home.

As I write these paragraphs many memories jostle each other to get my attention, and I realize what a significant influence Dr. Cummings has been on my life.

Fortunately, he had a great sense of humor. He needed it with me on his staff. Never once did he suggest that I go into veterinary medicine, and for good reason. I didn't exactly demonstrate the necessary gifts. But with grace and good humor he overlooked my blunders. Even the time I tried to spay a male cat.

Cats were undoubtedly my biggest problem; I simply never trusted the critters and they knew it. One day an unusually foul-spirited feline was brought to us by its proud owner. I didn't think there was much hope for a cure, inasmuch as we didn't do psychiatry, but I admitted the unwilling patient and somehow managed to get him into a cage.

The animal held me personally responsible for his misfortune.

Whenever I stepped into his line of sight he would hiss and snarl and lunge at me. Given the chance, he would have happily ripped my eyes out. The bars of the cage were my only protection.

So it was definitely not the high point of my life when Dr. Cummings asked me to get Mad Morris so we could work on him. I would have preferred his expeditious departing to wherever dead cats go, but how could I argue with my boss? I wasn't really afraid of losing my job. It had more to do with courage—my lack of it, specifically. How could I admit my fear to a man who daily battled problems far worse than mean cats? No, I had to try it. I had to open that cage door and grab that wriggling bundle of black terror.

Easier said than done. I tried everything I could think of, but his claws wouldn't let me get close enough even to unlatch the door. Just as I was ready to quit, feeling like a whipped puppy with tail dragging, I heard the gruff voice of Dr. Kraft, a veterinarian who regularly stopped by to help with difficult problems. My problem definitely qualified. I hated to admit I needed help, but I decided it beat the alternative.

With the confidence of a man who had handled animals for thirty years, Dr. Kraft assessed the situation and then asked me to find a light-weight rope. That was one task I could handle. With it, he tied a lasso.

"Now, open the door as quickly as you can," he said. As I jerked open the door, he tossed his little lariat like a seasoned cowboy roping a bad bull, and before the cat knew what had happened he was hanging from a noose with his life flashing before him.

The rapid approach of death effectively put Morris in a subdued state, and Dr. Kraft, not wanting to cut short the time for reflection and repentance, seemed in no hurry to offer clemency to the criminal.

"Don," he said, with a wry expression on his face and the cat still dangling from his rope, "you must first get the patient's attention."

Sometimes that's what God needs to do with us; sometimes he uses our afflictions as an opportunity to get our attention in order to quiet us enough for his healing. If we could find all the fulfillment we need in life through hard work and positive thinking, through snarling at all obstacles and clawing our way to happiness, we wouldn't need God. We could remain centered in ourselves, trusting our own sufficiency, and keep God at the periphery of our existence. We would then be living through the most absurd of all ironies, for we would be like Mad Morris fighting against the only physician able to cure our most serious sickness.

Charles Cummings wrote,

> The immediate supernatural usefulness of affliction is to teach me how poor, vulnerable, needy, naked, and fragile I really am. I imagine I am something, whereas in fact I am nothing (see Gal. 6:3). Without suffering I would go on living in the complacent illusion of having it all together and being on top of it all, through skillful management and superior preparation. The hurt that shatters that illusion is useful because it collapses the house of cards my ego has painstakingly erected and carefully held in balance. The shock of being badly hurt is enough to bring the whole structure down on my head and leave me exposed to the sun, the rain, and the wind.[8]

The pain of unfulfillment, then, signals to us that all is not right. Through it God gets our attention. "God whispers to us in our pleasures," C. S. Lewis wrote, "speaks in our conscience, but shouts in our pains: it is His megaphone to rouse a deaf world."[9]

When the truth finally gets through to us that we are not sufficient in ourselves to satisfy our deepest desires, the healing can begin.

We will know that we must leave the land of self-centered dreams and go home. We who have hitchhiked our way to this far country, like the runaway son Jesus told about, eventually find ourselves knee deep in pig slop. But when we come to ourselves, when we see ourselves as we really are—hungry and tired and helpless—we just might remember where to find at least one square meal a day. What we actually receive is so much more than we want but just what we need. We are embraced by a loving Father. He orders the servants to fetch the best set of clothes in the house, gives us the family seal-ring from his finger and sends out to Florsheim for brogues. We are decked out like models from *Esquire* or *Vogue,* the fattest calf on the ranch is turned into breaded veal, the stereo is turned up and the nails are jolted out of the floor by the dancing. The prodigals go from the pigpen to the party; the pain comes first and then the healing.

### Power in Weakness

Runaways who return home can be given much because they have nothing. Walking into the Father's front yard, they're a sorry sight: their clothes are indecent rags, their personal authority as bare as their blistered feet, their stomachs howling with hunger. So the Father gives them robes and rings and shoes and feasts. In the far country, when things were going well, they had no need of these things. But then came famine, and want made them beggars. Now they're ready for help.

Augustine said, "God wants to give us something but cannot because our hands are full—there's nowhere for Him to put it."[10] We often misjudge our deepest needs; we think we need a miraculous healing or an exciting relationship or a new house or any of the other wants that stoke the fires of discontent. Sometimes we manage to grasp these things, but our desperate clinging to them is like trying to hold water: we are left with nothing but a tightfisted emptiness. With hands closed we cannot receive the only thing that will really satisfy, the only thing that can get us through Saturday's suffering into Sunday's healing. We cannot receive the presence of God. But dead dreams and insufferable circumstances can open us to this essential gift by stripping clean our hands of all lesser goods that tempt us into a self-satisfied complacency.

God's presence in our lives is the work of the Holy Spirit. Now, some might feel a slight nervousness over the mention of the Holy Spirit. This could be because the King James Version of the Bible, the translation most of us grew up with, uses the term *Holy Ghost*—and ghosts are scary! The Holy Spirit, however, is nothing to be afraid of. The Spirit, who was active in creation, brings order out of the chaos of our lives. The Spirit, who dwelt fully in Jesus Christ, empowers us for ministry on behalf of the kingdom. The Spirit, who eternally binds together Father and Son in perfect love, holds us tightly in the holy embrace. When the risen Jesus breathed on his disciples and said, "Receive the Holy Spirit," he was giving them his power, the power of God, to enable them to be his people in the world. We could say that the Spirit specializes in getting us through Saturday, in keeping us moving along the often difficult road between the cross of Friday and the consummation of Sunday.

The emptiness of unfulfillment becomes the sphere in which the Spirit works. What we experience as unwelcome weakness becomes the occasion for the Spirit's welcome presence. This, too, is the good news of brokenness. Barren lives leave plenty of room for the Spirit's operation. "Blessed are the poor in spirit," Jesus said, "for theirs is the kingdom of heaven" (Mt 5:3). Blessed are those who feel like spiritual beggars, who feel like bums on a spiritual skid row, because they aren't too proud for a handout. They've given up on themselves.

The copper coins of human success have long since fallen through their holey pockets, and now they're ready for the gold coin of holy power.

It's important to point out that the Spirit doesn't transform our weakness into power. The Spirit doesn't nurture us like a mother until we're weaned from her breasts and eventually strong enough to feed our own hunger. No, our weakness remains; we continue in dependency. We will often *feel* weak in our Christian life, though we live by faith and have been given the Spirit, because in fact we *are* weak. But the Spirit manifests God's power in the midst of our weakness.

Nowhere do we see this more clearly than in the correspondence Paul had with the church in Corinth. The Spirit of God was clearly present in that fellowship of believers, but so also was a spirit of pride. People were comparing spiritual attainments like Boy Scouts displaying "signs and wonders" merit badges on puffed out chests. Had you tried to join that church you probably would have felt like a spiritual pygmy trying to dance with giants, and you would have bumped your nose against their holier-than-thou kneecaps as they pointed out some pretty impressive stuff—healings and prophecies and ecstatic tongues.

They didn't think much of Paul. He was powerful with a pen, they thought, but unimpressive in person. A saying concerning Paul began to circulate through the network of church gossip: "His letters are weighty and strong, but his bodily presence is weak, and his speech of no account" (2 Cor 10:10). Paul's authority was threatened; the Corinthians couldn't understand how a man with his obvious weaknesses could really be an apostle.

Paul defended himself in a surprising way. Instead of covering his failures with a mound of reported successes, he buried his successes under a mountain of admitted failures. He could have told them of answers to prayer, no doubt, and given some impressive statistics about conversions and new church developments. But he did the unexpected: he gloried in his weakness. In the second letter, for example, he began by referring to his afflictions and sufferings eight times in less than six verses (1:3-8), ending this litany of woe with the stark confession, "we felt that we had received the sentence of death" (1:9). F. Dale Bruner has called Paul's theology in 2 Corinthians a "theology of death." "But it is a death (a sense of radical weakness) which one knows in oneself in order that God may give life and receive the honor."[11]

> Paul seems to be saying: "If I were personally impressive or overwhelming, if you did see me bristling with power, what would make me any different from any other powerful, impressive personality in the world? As it is, you see me in all my weaknesses, in this "earthen vessel," but this is exactly where God can be God. You can know the power in my ministry is God's because you can trace so little of it in me. The way I am you can be sure 'that the transcendent power belongs to God and not to me' " (2 Cor 4:7).[12]

At one point in his correspondence Paul did "boast" about a spiritual experience, a vision which took him to the "third heaven" (2 Cor 12:2), but immediately, as if to keep things in proper balance, he said, "A thorn was given me in the flesh" (2 Cor 12:7). Who knows what it was? Maybe no one but God ever knew; maybe it was too embarrassing to mention; maybe it was so well known he didn't need to belabor the obvious. In any event, it made life hard. So Paul did what we ought always to do with thorny problems: he prayed. He asked for relief.

Once, twice, three times he banged on the door of heaven. But nothing happened. The door opened not a crack. The thorn remained firmly buried in his flesh.

Something else opened for him, though. He entered into a new understanding, a deeper faith. He learned that though there may be many things you can do without, there is one thing you cannot do without, one thing that so transcends everything else in importance it can scarcely be compared to them.

The one thing he discovered in the midst of his suffering, and maybe only because of his suffering, was this: God's grace is sufficient. Sufficient for what? He didn't say. Perhaps that silence itself was his point. Just sufficient. Period. God's grace doesn't confer automatic success or spiritual razzle dazzle. Its results may not be outwardly impressive. It certainly doesn't overcome all weakness. But it is sufficient. God provides enough of his presence—the Holy Spirit—to make it possible to endure. Enough to keep you going on the journey though you've stumbled and bloodied your knees. Enough to empower your weakness for an effective ministry. Enough to keep your eyes on the distant horizon though it's too dark to see much of anything else. Yes, God sometimes gives us exactly what we ask for, but often the answers to prayer we receive are the same as Paul's—the sufficiency of grace.

Paul's theology of the Christian life and ministry came directly from the cross of Christ. Nowhere was weakness more obvious, nowhere defeat more evident. But God was in that weakness, and through it he revealed his power of salvation for the world.

**Chiseled into Masterpieces**
The suffering of unfulfillment can be used by God for our ultimate good. He uses it as a tool to get our attention and as an opportunity to manifest his power in weakness. One final point needs to be

made before this chapter ends: God also uses suffering to transform us into the image of Christ.

Sin has left its mark on us; self-centeredness has marred our true humanity. Calvinist theologians speak of our "total depravity." They don't mean by this phrase that we have nothing good in us, but rather that sin has damaged the core of our being. If you start buttoning a shirt by putting the first button in the wrong hole, you will finish amiss no matter how well you complete the task. In the same way, if you live out of self-centeredness, you—the final you—will always end up wrong. A heart turned in upon itself creates a bent person. Much good and beauty may be left, but your person-hood *as a whole* will not be good and beautiful.

According to the Bible, we're all in this condition. "Since all have sinned and fall short of the glory of God" (Rom 3:23). No exceptions. Not only do we fall short of God's glory, we fall short of our own true glory. God intended more for us; at creation he bestowed on us the dignity of his image. But we've damaged the goods and we're a sorry semblance of the real thing.

So as part of his continuing grace toward us, God has resolved to restore the image we've destroyed and discarded. In Jesus Christ he not only provides a means to forgive the vandalism of our sin, but also provides a model of our new humanity, the prototype of the new image he is creating for us. We are "predestined to be conformed to the image of his Son, in order that he might be the first-born among many brethren" (Rom 8:29). And when God pre-destines something, you can count on it; he has the creative re-sources to finish the task. Thus we are even now, whether we realize it or not, "being changed into his likeness from one degree of glory to another; for this comes from the Lord who is the Spirit" (2 Cor 3:18). In spite of Saturday's suffering and often because of it, the day has this greatness: God the Holy Spirit is transforming us into the image of Jesus Christ.

I like to think of God as a great sculptor. His artistry with us will one day make Michelangelo's "David" look like a discarded blunder from a kindergarten art class. But to complete the work he has much to do.

Throughout most of history, sculptors have used basically two techniques: carving and modeling. In carving, a sculptor starts with a block of wood or stone and, visualizing the finished figure, cuts and chips away the material until only the desired image remains. In modeling, the artist builds up his sculpture by adding layers of clay or wax or some other substance. God utilizes both techniques, chiseling away sin and reshaping with the clay of a Christlike character.

The first part hurts—when the chisel's sharp edge cuts through the hardened desire of a determined will. Because self-centeredness is the very thing which needs to be gouged out of our lives, disappointment is often the most useful tool in the hands of the Master Craftsman, the chisel with the necessary weight and bevel to do the work. Growth into Christlikeness often depends on our not getting our way. When the hammer of God's no pounds the wedge of frustrated longing deep into our being, a piece of egocentricity breaks off and we come that much closer to being a masterpiece.

And then the Craftsman fills in gaps and smooths over rough places and holds together broken pieces—he reshapes us—with the clay of a new Christlikeness. God the Holy Spirit works within us, changing our characters. Paul told the Christians in Galatia that "the fruit of the Spirit is love, joy, peace, patience, kindness, goodness, faithfulness, gentleness, self-control" (Gal 5:22-23). These words describe the result of the Spirit's presence and perfectly portray the

---

**156**

character of Jesus Christ, according to whose image we are being transformed.

When will the artist be finished? When will we finally become masterpieces? Not until Sunday. Not until our Lord consummates his saving work and we stand face to face with him in glory. "We know that when he appears we shall be like him, for we shall see him as he is" (1 Jn 3:2). "Just as we have borne the image of the man of dust, we shall also bear the image of the man of heaven" (1 Cor 15:49).

Until then, it's Saturday still, and the cloud-shrouded sun has yet to set before rising anew in Sunday's splendor.

## Discussion Questions

1. What is *character*? What are all the ways one's character is influenced and developed?

2. When we face adversity, how does James's injunction to "consider it all joy" differ from the more common motto "when the going get's tough, the tough get going"? What does it really mean to face our struggles with joy?

3. Look back over the suffering you have experienced in your life. How have these experiences changed you? How has God used them?

4. Do you know people who demonstrate Christ's power because they are weak in themselves? Whom? Has this ever been your experience? When?

5. Why is weakness and lack of control such a threatening feeling? How does it make you feel knowing you will never overcome your dependence on the Spirit and that God wants it that way?

# CHAPTER ELEVEN

# Disciplines
# for
# Living
# with
# God

The last chapter announced some good news: *God can use the broken-ness of life to make us whole.*

Now we need to think about our own responsibility, the role we must play in this healing. The rain may fall on many different fields, but only the wise farmer who has dug his ditches will make the best use of it. How do we open ourselves to the work of God?

It will take, in a word, discipline. There will be times when we'd rather not pick up the shovel, times when the blisters hurt, times when we despair of ever finishing the job and times when we're too weary to care anymore. But as W. C. Fields put it, "There comes a time in the affairs of humanity when you must take the bull by the tail and face the situation!"[1] Whether we like what's in front of us or not, we can no longer ignore it. Life makes some hard demands. One of them is that if we wish to live well and survive the pains of disappointment, we must face the often unpleasant necessity of discipline.

Paradoxically, freedom emerges only from self-constraint; liberty lives only in the land of law. The great composer Igor Stravinsky wrote, "My freedom will be so much the greater and more meaningful the more narrowly I limit my field of action and the more I surround myself with obstacles. Whatever diminishes constraint, diminishes strength. The more constraints one imposes, the more one frees oneself of the chains that shackle the spirit."[2] And Karl Barth wrote that Mozart "moved freely within the limits of the musical laws of his time. . . . But he did not revolt against these laws; he did not break them. He sought to be himself and yet achieved his greatness precisely in being himself while observing the conventions which he imposed upon himself."[3]

Achievements in any area of life require discipline. An athlete never wins the prize, a businesswoman never becomes vice president, a scholar never writes a good book, an artist never creates beauty—without discipline. This is obvious.

But what seems not so obvious to many is that this principle also applies to the emotional and spiritual realms of life. Here we often act, for some strange reason, according to a perverted notion of freedom—doing what we like, when we like, with no challenge to our comfort—which we expect will carry us effortlessly through the desert of unfulfillment into the bliss of happiness.

It doesn't work that way. "Do not be deceived," Paul warned the Christians in Galatia, "God is not mocked, for whatever a man sows, that he will also reap. For he who sows to his own flesh will from the flesh reap corruption; but he who sows to the Spirit will from the Spirit reap eternal life" (Gal 6:7-8). If you want to fly with the eagles or keep pace with the runners or even just walk with the weary, you must regularly exercise the muscles and tendons of faith.

What, specifically, are the constraints we must impose on ourselves if we are to compose a music of living? What can we do to open ourselves to the power of God which brings wholeness out of brokenness? In this chapter and the next I will list some important disciplines which can help us live more productively and peacefully with the problems of unfulfillment. By committing ourselves to these practices we allow God to shape us into the image of his Son.

## The Discipline of a Devotional Life

Once I rented a sailboat in the hope of making enjoyable use of a stiff wind blowing across Seattle's Green Lake. The only vessel available from the boathouse was a broken-down boat with no centerboard. I should have known better than to take it, but my desire for adventure overpowered my good sense. Adventure quickly slid into terror as my boat slid out of control. I rammed a dock and nearly capsized before I nervously navigated back to the boathouse. Sailboats need centerboards.

Our lives, too, need centerboards for stability. The discipline of a devotional life meets this need. It helps prevent the winds of desire from blowing us across the surface of things; it stabilizes our keel, enabling us to make the best possible use of those winds, even the ones beating hard against our bow.

There are two parts to the practice of disciplined devotion: weekly worship and daily prayer.

Earlier I stressed the importance of worship, the turning of ourselves away from the petty gods of materialism, power and religion to the God revealed in Jesus Christ. Through worship God draws us *out of* ourselves and thus saves us *from* ourselves.

Because of its significance, worship cannot be left to the vagaries of feeling. It must be structured into our lives with a rhythm of time and place. The reason for this is not because we can worship properly only on Sunday mornings in the company of God's people. Surely we can and should worship God on the golf course or at the beach or even with our head resting on a pillow. But we make worship a ritual for at least two reasons.

First, by setting aside a specific time and place for worship we clearly show what is true about all times and all places. You enjoy a wedding anniversary in a romantic restaurant, for example, not because that's the only time you love and appreciate your spouse but because you want to celebrate what you feel at all times (well, at least at most times). Or you throw a birthday party for a friend, not because that's the only time you care deeply for her but because you want to show the affection you have throughout the year. Even so, we join with others Sunday by Sunday at ten o'clock in the brick building at Fifth and Main, not because we can't worship God anywhere else, but because we can and do, and we want to make that clear to ourselves and to our world.

Second, we make worship a ritual because of its value for us. Now, most of us don't feel friendly toward the word *ritual*. We speak of "dead ritual" or "empty ritual" or "hollow ritual"; ritual seems like a scaffolding elaborately erected around nothing. But I suggest the opposite is true: we create rituals out of the things we really value.

Every morning after getting out of bed, I shower, pour a cup of coffee, read the Bible, pray, read the newspaper and go to my office. These are all rituals—precisely because I greatly value them. I have structured certain things into my life because they reflect my commitment to be a certain kind of person.

Is there anyone who doesn't live by rituals? We all do, and it's a good thing. We need them. Some rituals, of course, are not good; mindless, unexamined rituals can constrict personal growth. But thoughtful, consciously chosen rituals can help liberate us. We should ritualize worship for this reason. Through it we can be released from the tyranny of self-centered desires and drawn into the presence of the God who makes all things new in Jesus Christ.

And we should make prayer a daily ritual. Prayer is too important to be stored in the basement of life, only to be pulled out and dusted off for the occasional emergency; it must take its place in the living room and bedroom and kitchen—in the regularly lived-in areas of life. "Pray constantly," Paul wrote to the Christians in Thessalonica (1 Thess 5:17). And he said as much to those in Rome: "Be constant in prayer" (Rom 12:12). And to those in Ephesus: "Pray at all times" (Eph 6:18). And to those in Colossae: "Continue steadfastly in prayer" (Col 4:2).

Certainly Paul didn't mean we should escape into a monastic world of calloused knees and constantly folded hands. We can't. The garbage must be taken out, diapers need changing and bills have to be paid. To pray constantly simply means that along with everything else we do, we ought also to pray. It is as necessary for our spirits as is brushing for our teeth. We should make prayer a daily ritual.

Why? Aren't there good reasons for *not* praying? We live in an age of increasing technological capabilities. Perhaps our ancestors needed to pray for rain, but today we water fields with computerized sprinklers. We get our healing from doctors and our daily bread from supermarkets. Why should we pray? Do not even our theological beliefs make prayer superfluous? Why pray if God is omniscient and knows what we need? Why pray if he is love and willing to give what we need?

There are three reasons for praying. First, God tells us to pray. Jesus taught that we "ought always to pray and not lose heart" (Lk 18:1), and the entire Bible witnesses to this necessity. We certainly don't understand all the laws of cause and effect in the universe, but we know this: God wants us to pray. And we would do well to trust him in this matter. When a doctor prescribes medication, we don't demand an exact explanation of the chemical and biological processes involved; we simply trust the doctor's knowledge and good will. The God who has shown his love in Jesus Christ has proven himself trustworthy.

The second reason we should pray is because our relationship with God demands it. By prayer we enter into fellowship with God. We don't pray as children hollering to a distracted or reluctant parent, trying to get God's attention or to get him to do what we want. We pray because we already have God's attention and good will, and by praying we allow ourselves to be shaped by his good purposes.

Finally, we pray because it makes a difference. "The prayer of a righteous man has great power in its effects" (Jas 5:16). Why this should be so, I don't know. But God, out of his abundant grace toward us, has chosen to rely on our prayers, to let them influence the way he relates to this world and to us. Harry Emerson Fosdick pointed out that if God has left some things contingent on human thinking and working, he surely could have left some things contingent on human praying. "We pray for the same reason that we work and think, because only so can the wise and good God get some things done which he wants done."[4] Perhaps some things need prayer because God can't give them unless we want them badly enough to ask; perhaps some things demand a receptive attitude, a hunger on our part. Whatever the reason, he invites our prayer and promises to answer. "Ask," said Jesus, "and it will be given you; seek, and you will find; knock, and it will be opened to you" (Mt 7:7).

"Pray constantly." You may not be in the mood, but pray anyway. You may feel like a spiritual nincompoop, but pray anyway. You may have a tongue tied tighter than a Boy Scout knot, but pray anyway. Pray anyway— because these feelings mean you're in the ideal condition for prayer. Augustine said, "The best disposition for praying is that of being desolate, forsaken, stripped of everything."[5]

## The Discipline of Listening

The second discipline through which we open ourselves to the work of God is by listening to the Word of God. When God speaks, something happens. Unlike human words, which often miss their target and fall to the ground like broken arrows, God's Word never fails to hit its mark. It not only *means* what it says, it *does* what it says; God's Word both announces and creates reality. God's Word is a creative event.

The creation story in the first chapter of the Bible has a refrain which strikes the reader's consciousness like waves pounding against the shore: "And God said . . . And God said . . . And God said . . ." God spoke creation into being. "And God said, 'Let there be light'; and there was light" (Gen 1:3), and so on through to the creation of man and woman. God spoke to nothing, and nothing sat up and became something. God's Word accomplishes what he purposes and prospers in the thing for which he sends it (Is 55:11). And of course this unity of announcement and act reached fulfillment when "the Word became flesh and dwelt among us, full of grace and truth" (Jn 1:14). Jesus is the Word of God, a Word which proclaims and establishes the truth of reconciliation.

To this Word of God we must listen, opening ourselves in expectation of a new creation. Where do we hear it? Though we cannot narrowly limit God's Word to certain spheres, since he remains sovereignly free, we can nonetheless say that he speaks primarily in three places: Scripture, sermon and sacraments.

The Word encounters us through the written word of the Scripture, through the prophetic and apostolic witness. The Bible is "the infallible rule of faith and practice" (Westminster Confession), not because the book fell directly from heaven into the church's lap, but because the infallible Christ continues to humble himself, using fallible human witnesses as instruments through which he summons to faith and discipleship.

And the Word encounters us through the spoken word of the sermon, through the proclamation of the Scripture. Dietrich Bonhoeffer, echoing the conviction of Augustine and Luther, wrote, "Christ is not only present *in* the Word of the Church, but also *as* the Word of the Church, that means the spoken Word of preaching. . . . Christ's presence is his existence as proclamation."[6] This doesn't mean that God inspires every word of every sermon. We've all heard some pretty bad sermons; some of us have even preached them. (I'm reminded of Mr. Phelps, the farmer-preacher described by Huck Finn, who "never charged nothing for his preaching. And it was worth it, too."[7]) Bonhoeffer means rather that Christ continues to humble himself, using the imperfect event of human speech to deliver his perfect Word of salvation.

And the Word encounters us through the visible word of the sacraments, through the acts of baptism and the Lord's Supper. In these little dramas symbolizing the great drama of redemption, Christ presents himself to us and confirms the reality of his gracious love. Here the Word, the truth spoken to us in the Christ who meets us, is more than something to hear; it can be touched. "The sacraments," Dale Bruner has said, "are God's hugs—they are God physically approaching and touching us."[8]

The creative, life-bringing Word comes to us in this threefold form of Scripture, sermon and sacraments. We must therefore practice the discipline of listening—*careful* listening. Our preconceptions must be set aside; our inner voices must be stilled; our hearts must be opened. Freeman Patterson, an outstanding Canadian photographer, explained his method of taking pictures in a way that describes well the openness we need in order to hear the Word of God:

On those frosty mornings when I grab my camera and tripod, and head out into the meadow behind the house, I quickly forget about me. I stop thinking about what I'll do with the photographs, or about self-fulfillment, and lose myself in the sheer magic of rainbows in the grass; in the multi-coloured prisms of back-lighted crystals. I am lost in a world of glittering lights and dancing colours. I experience myself in what I see, and the result is a tremendous exuberance which helps me make the best use of my camera, and which lasts long after the frost has melted.

Letting go of the self is an essential precondition to real seeing. When you let go of yourself, you abandon any preconceptions about the subject matter which might cramp you into photographing in a certain, predetermined way. As long as you are worried about whether or not you will be able to make good pictures, or are concerned about enjoying yourself, you are unlikely either to take the best photographs you can or experience the joy of photography to the fullest. When you let go new conceptions arise from your direct experience of the subject matter, and new ideas and feelings will guide you as you make pictures.

Preoccupation with self is the greatest barrier to seeing, and the hardest one to break.[9]

Preoccupation with self is also the greatest barrier to hearing. We must discipline ourselves to silence the cacophonous voices of screaming desire and lamenting unfulfillment long enough to hear the Word which can create all things new again.

### The Discipline of Obedience

Through the disciplines of devotion and careful listening, we hear the Living Word say to us, "Follow me." In that instant we are faced with a choice: to obey or not to obey. "The word that is translated *follow* in most instances in the Gospel is rooted in the Greek word for road. To follow is to share the same road. The Christian's prayer is not for a longer stay with God but for a closer walk with God."[10] We obey when we follow God down the road he is walking, and we disobey when we walk down a road of our own choosing.

There are good reasons for not obeying. We don't know what might await us at the end of God's road; we often see only the next step we must take. For this reason the alternatives can seem very inviting. Though we actually have no more knowledge of where the roads of our own choosing will lead, we *think* they will lead to an imagined happiness. A woman, for example, supposes she has found a way out of her barren loneliness when she meets a man with whom she shares a mutual attraction. Never mind that he is married to someone else. The romance feels so right; surely this road leads out of her unfulfillment into a garden of pleasure. But then the Word confronts her, and suddenly she finds herself at a crossroads. As far as she can see down one road the way appears clear and the scenery beautiful. Down the other road she sees nothing but more of the wilderness she is in. But from this unpromising road there comes a voice calling, "Follow me."

There is only one reason for obeying. God has proven himself trustworthy through his love in Jesus Christ. Faith leads to obedience. Twice in his letter to the Roman Christians Paul wrote of "the obedience of faith" (Rom 1:5; 16:26). Faithful hearts create obedient wills. When I entrust my life to God I will follow where he leads, as a child naturally follows a loving parent. I may not always understand why I'm led down certain roads; I may not know what's around the next bend or over the next mountain; I may not always find it easy to follow. But if I believe he loves me with a perfect wisdom, I must trust him to lead in the best possible way.

The most difficult roads of obedience often offer the greatest opportunities for growth. The author of Hebrews wrote of Jesus: "Although he was a Son, he learned obedience through what he suffered; and being made perfect he became the source of eternal salvation to all who obey him" (Heb 5:8-9). Jesus himself was somehow perfected by obediently walking down a road which led to a Roman cross. Now if the Son of God needed his obedience tested through such suffering, can we reasonably expect to travel at all times on roads of ease? The way of obedience may not always be easy but it alone leads to spiritual maturity.

### The Discipline of Gratitude

One of the most effective medicines for treating the pain of unmet desire is gratitude. The cup may be half-empty but we can drink it like a Thanksgiving toast.

Gratitude can turn our world upside down. A change of perspective can happen for us when we give thanks for what we do have rather than let ourselves be overwhelmed by what we do not have. This book has tried to face honestly the reality of unfulfillment, and I'm not now trying to minimize it. But even the shallowest pond has *some* water in it; life is not totally dry for any of us. When we practice the discipline of gratitude we begin to understand an important truth: nothing *has* to be. We may not have all we'd like to have, but what we do enjoy is a gift from God.

John Claypool, a Baptist pastor, has written a moving testimony to his experience with a great loss. His eight-year-old daughter, Laura Lue, was diagnosed as having acute leukemia. Eighteen months later she was dead. Claypool had ministered to many people in times of tragedy. Now the pain was marching through his heart like Hitler's troops going through Poland. No cheap and easy comfort came. But he was helped when he came to understand that all life is a gift.

At least it makes things bearable when I remember that Laura Lue was a gift, pure and simple, something I neither earned nor deserved nor had a right to. And when I remember that the appropriate response to a gift, even when it is taken away, is gratitude, then I am better able to try and thank God that I was ever given her in the first place. . . . Believe me, the only way out is the way of gratitude. The way of remorse does not alter the stark reality one whit and only makes matters worse. The way of gratitude does not alleviate the pain, but it somehow puts some light around the darkness and builds strength to begin to move on.[11]

Let me offer some very practical advice: start your prayers with thanksgiving. Thank God for his gifts before mentioning your needs. Don't begin with confession of sin (you may not have time for anything else), and don't begin with petition (your own needs will dominate your thinking). Instead, enter into God's presence with thanksgiving (Ps 95:2). I have tried to practice this simple discipline of gratitude for many years, and I have found it helpful in providing a more balanced perspective—especially when the longing for unmet desires starts to control my feelings and thinking.

As the Nazis gained control of Germany, Dietrich Bonhoeffer had every reason to despair over the scarcity of authentic faith in a church which was making one compromise after another until the Swastika literally draped its altars. In 1938 he wrote a little book which grew out of his experiences as the head of an underground seminary for the Confessing Church. Given the situation in which he wrote, his words are surprising:

> In the Christian community thankfulness is just what it is anywhere else in the Christian life. Only he who gives thanks for little things receives the big things. We prevent God from giving us the great spiritual gifts he has in store for us, because we do not give thanks for daily gifts. We think we dare not be satisfied with the small measure of spiritual knowledge, experience, and love that has been given to us, and that we must constantly be looking forward eagerly for the highest good. Then we deplore the fact that we lack the deep certainty, the strong faith, and the rich experience that God has given to others, and we consider this lament to be pious. We pray for the big things and forget to give thanks for the ordinary, small (and yet really not small) gifts. How can God entrust great things to one who will not thankfully receive from him the little things? If we do not give thanks daily for the Christian fellowship in which we have been placed, even where there is no great experience, no discoverable riches, but much weakness, small faith, and difficulty; if, on the contrary, we

only keep complaining to God that everything is so paltry and petty, so far from what we expected, then we hinder God from letting our fellowship grow according to the measure and riches which are there for us all in Jesus Christ.[12]

Bonhoeffer realized that nothing has to be. The pains of unfulfillment could be eased in a significant way if we would come to the same understanding. All life is God's gracious gift, and thus our instinctive response should be gratitude—even if what we have seems weak and of no account.

**The Discipline of Being Open to God's Surprises**

When the pain of unfulfillment cries out for immediate relief, it usually asks for a specific kind of relief. Our longing imagines a concrete fulfillment. A man wants his hunger for intimacy satisfied not simply with any woman but with a particular kind of woman. A woman wants to achieve not simply any worthwhile objective but the one tenaciously held by her dreams. Our hopes don't hover like ghosts in an ethereal realm; they materialize into definite shapes. And when the future doesn't seem to be unfolding according to our precise desires, we may find our anxiety increasing and our faith faltering.

This rising anxiety we feel is nothing other than a crisis of confidence in the infinite creativity of God.

The God revealed in Jesus Christ is a God of surprises. Abraham and Sarah laughed till the tears ran down their cheeks when an angel announced that the stork was on its way. Who could have guessed such a thing? Abraham had celebrated a hundred birthdays and Sarah was only a decade behind him. Of course they laughed. "Sarah and her husband had had plenty of hard knocks in their time, and there were plenty more of them still to come, but at that moment when the angel told them they'd better start dipping into their old age pensions for cash to build a nursery, the reason they laughed was that it suddenly dawned on them that the wildest dreams they'd ever had hadn't been half wild enough."[13]

When God fulfilled the covenant he had made with Abraham and his descendants, who could have guessed the twists in the story? The Son of God made his appearance not in a royal palace but in a crude stable, and he was carried to his death not on the laments of a loving people but on the disgrace of a criminal's cross. And if the end of that chapter surprised his disciples, the start of the next blew them out of their sandals. The one who had been defeated, proven wrong by thorns and nails and the cold of the tomb, appeared to them and declared his authority over all things.

The surprises weren't finished for his followers. Peter happily preached the good news to the Jews until he was sent kicking and screaming to the house of Cornelius, where he watched the Holy Spirit descend on Gentiles. Saul, the most aggressive persecutor of Christians, became Paul, the greatest apostle of the church. Augustine's mother prayed all night in a seaside chapel on the coast of north Africa, begging God not to let her son sail for Italy where surely he would stray far beyond hope of redemption; he sailed, and in Italy he met Ambrose who led him to Christ. Luther simply hoped to discuss a few matters, possibly hold a seminar with interested students, when he posted his Ninety-Five theses on the door of the Castle Church in Wittenberg, and then he found himself leading a reformation. Calvin wanted to be left alone to do his scholarly work, but instead became the father of the Reformed wing of Protestantism. Phillips Brooks decided to be a teacher but, failing at that, became what many believe was the greatest American preacher of the nineteenth century. Adoniram Judson set his heart on being a missionary to India, but couldn't get in; he went instead to Burma, where he established the country's first church, translated the Bible and inspired thousands of others to take the gospel where it had not been heard before.

When doors of desire slam in your face, trust the creativity of God to open new, unexpected doors into the future. To be open takes discipline, a dedicated expectancy, a trust that anything at all is possible with the God who can turn the tragedy of Good Friday into the triumph of Easter.

## Discussion Questions

1. Why does the Christian life take discipline?

2. We create rituals out of the things we really value. What things have you elevated into rituals? How can you make prayer and worship a structured part of your life?

3. What is prayer? Why should we pray? How often do you pray? What barriers do you face that hinder you from praying more?

4. Think of a time when you noticed that someone was really listening to you. What did they do that communicated that they were good listeners? How can we become good listeners of God's voice? What, if anything, keeps you from listening to God?

5. What do you first think of when you hear the word *obedience?* Was it a positive or a negative image? Explain. If you decided to let all your defenses down and obey God unconditionally, what do you think would happen? How would your life change?

6. How do the disciplines of gratitude and flexibility help us to deal with the ups and downs of life? What would our lives be like without these disciplines?

# CHAPTER TWELVE

# Disciplines
# for Living
# in a
# Broken
# World

Through practicing the disciplines discussed in the last chapter, we open ourselves up to the power of God. These disciplines are not steps by which we ascend into heaven to get God's attention. God has already come near to us in Jesus Christ and promised to strengthen us with his Spirit; he is the God of grace. Through these disciplines we receive what he wants to give us.

And then we must carry on in this world. Life on Saturday, though filled with the hope of an approaching Sunday, still limps and aches from the wounds of sin. The following disciplines, then, are designed to help us deal with the brokenness in which we live.

### The Discipline of Accepting Incompleteness

Life has as many loose ends as a half-knit sweater. Experiences often dangle about us, seemingly unconnected to a meaningful pattern: a relationship once treasured, now lost; a marital union severed by death; a once-promising career abandoned; a mountain-top experience towering above the flat terrain of everyday spirituality. What do these mean in relationship to one another? How will the strands ever intertwine into a complete, presentable garment?

We'd like to be able to leave a clean desk at the end of the day, with everything filed away and all tasks completed and not so much as a stray paper clip out of place, but we can't pull it off. Life is too untidy.

Recently a young woman telephoned to share with me the heartwrenching news that her five-year-old son has muscular dystrophy. In the conversation she said, "And I still haven't gotten over the death of my father nearly twenty years ago. If I could only know what it all means. . . . What's God trying to do with me?"

We tend to think life would be more liveable—more endurable—if somehow we could see the final meaning of things. But we can't, at least not now. The approach of Sunday promises us that eventually "we shall understand fully." But "now we see in a mirror dimly" (1 Cor 13:12), and thus the realities of Saturday demand that we learn to live with incompleteness. This takes discipline. We need to consistently remind ourselves that broken people in a broken world will always be lacerated by the fragments and ragged edges of life.

Eugene Peterson ends a book on the prophet Jeremiah with these wise paragraphs:

Flannery O'Connor once remarked that she had an aunt who thought that nothing happened in a story unless somebody got married or shot at the end of it. But life seldom provides such definitive endings. . . . Life is ambiguous. There are loose ends. It takes maturity to live with the ambiguity and the chaos, the absurdity and the untidiness. If we refuse to live with it, we exclude something, and what we exclude may very well be the essential and dear—the hazards of faith, the mysteries of God.

Jeremiah ends inconclusively. We want to know the end, but there is no end. The last scene of Jeremiah's life shows him, as he had spent so much of his life, preaching God's word to a contemptuous people (Jer 44). We want to know that he was finally successful so that, if we live well and courageously, we also will be successful. Or we want to know that he was finally unsuccessful so that, since a life of faith and integrity doesn't pay off, we can go on with finding another means by which to live. We get neither in Jeremiah. He doesn't get married and he doesn't get shot. In Egypt, the place he doesn't want to be, with people who treat him badly, he continues determinedly faithful, magnificently courageous, heartlessly rejected—a towering life terrifically lived.[1]

May it be so for us, too, living in our own Egypt of incompleteness.

### The Discipline of Failing Forward

Life is risky. Getting through it can be like walking across a mine field; the next step could blow your world apart. It seems that God has ordered things so that the greatest joys (loving relationships, creative work, meaningful service) bring with them the greatest risks for failure.

And we do fail. All of us, without exception. Some failure we bring upon ourselves; some we suffer from without. No one escapes the pain of striking out before the season's end. Bitter memories rise up in accusation when we survey the past, and fearful anticipations threaten when we imagine the future. We have to admit, with Pogo, that "we have faults we haven't even used yet," and those faults lie in wait, like criminals, ready to ambush us.

What will we do with failure? We have a choice. Either we can withdraw, or we can learn the discipline of failing forward.

After being burned you naturally want to stay away from fire. If taking risks means getting hurt, it might seem better to play it safe. Every counselor has seen this. A man's heart has just been torn apart by a failed romance and he says, with bitterness, "I'm never going to be such a fool again," and he sets about barricading himself against any future emotional involvement. Or a woman's first attempt at creativity receives a cool reception which to her feels like rejection, and she retreats back into the boring but safe world of the familiar. For some it seems better to accept the known pain of unfulfillment than to risk the unknown pain of seeking greater fulfillment.

But withdrawing never works. Paul Tillich once said, "He who risks and fails can be forgiven. He who never risks and never fails is a failure in his whole being." To be fully human we must engage life—we must make decisions, build relationships, create beauty, give ourselves. Not to take these risks is the greatest risk of all, the risk of losing our humanity. The way Jesus told it, the villain is the one who plays it safe by burying his treasure in the back yard, and the hero is the one who doubles his money by laying it all down on Blessed Dreamer in the sixth (my paraphrase, Mt 25:14-30). Life demands risk, and risk entails failure.

Thus we must learn to fail well. Strange as it may sound, you can fail at failing or you can succeed at failing. Thomas Watson was once asked the secret of his success in bringing IBM to its place of leadership in the computer industry. Watson replied, "I have learned how to fail forward!" That's the secret of failing well.

One summer of my boyhood, while visiting a favorite uncle and aunt, I was taken to a dairy. I wasn't much interested in cows but had high hopes for the outing because Uncle Thom knew how to have a good time. It looked as if he would outdo his own standards of excellence when he disappeared into a shed and wheeled out an old motorcycle. My eyes were as big as its wheels when he revved the engine and said to me, "Take it away!" You can imagine the thrill. The years have not robbed me of the exhilarating feeling of power and speed and wind blowing in my face. I hadn't been riding a bicycle very long, and now a motorcycle! It was great fun. Until I crashed.

Dirt flew around me like a Midwestern tornado, the engine screamed angrily, and my knee throbbed with pain. Through the smoky, bloody confusion I could see Uncle Thom running toward me, and my heart sank in embarrassment and self-disgust.

Before I could say anything he said, "Get up and get back on it." I wasn't as excited about the opportunity this time. But he knew that I had to put my failure behind me or be paralyzed by it in the future. So with some nervousness I was off again, taking the turns a bit more slowly and keeping a closer watch on the road. I had fallen, but with Uncle Thom's help I had fallen forward.

When Jesus sent his disciples out to preach and raise the dead and do all manner of marvelous ministry, he prepared them for failure. "And if any one will not receive you or listen to your words," he said, "shake off the dust from your feet as you leave that house or town" (Mt 10:14). You win some and lose some—even if you're a disciple. So shake off the dust of failure and move on. Fail forward.

I wonder if Peter thought of those words in a very different context, at a time of personal failure. He had blown it; he had hit the dust so hard he had more failure to shake off than could be hauled away in a dump truck. At a crucial moment, when his master needed him most, Peter betrayed him. "The Rock" became shifting sand by denying he even knew the one he had so recently called the Son of the living God. Peter left Jesus alone—totally alone to face a hostile world.

By the time this story was recorded Peter's name was known throughout the church; he had been the foremost apostle, the leader of earliest Christians. We might have expected the story of his denial to have been hushed up, kindly forgotten out of respect for the great man. But no. This is one of few events recorded in all four of the Gospels. It seems the church went out of its way to remember the day Peter fell flat on his face in failure. Why? Perhaps to remind itself that if it could happen to Peter it could happen to anyone. And perhaps to remind itself of God's grace which can empty tombs of dead regret by the power of new beginnings.

It would be good to remind ourselves of these things, too, as we practice the discipline of failing forward.

### The Discipline of Serving Others

Dr. Karl Menninger, the well-known psychiatrist, once lectured on mental health and then opened it to questions from the audience. "What would you advise a person to do," asked one man, "if that person felt a nervous breakdown coming on?" Perhaps most expected him to say, "Consult a psychiatrist." But he replied, "Lock up your house, go across the railway tracks, find someone in need and do something to help that person."[2]

One of the best things you can do when the pain of unfulfillment throws you to the mat is to practice the discipline of serving others.

No doubt, you may not feel like it; you may think you need help with your own hurt; you may wonder how someone like you, who feels as dry as an Arizona mesa in August, could possibly quench another's thirst. But the effort of focusing on needs outside yourself can give you the proper perspective on the needs inside yourself, and it can provide a kind of rest for the unfulfilled part of your being, as if the muscles of longing were given a break from their strenuous work.

Harold Kushner tells an old Chinese tale about a woman whose only son died. She asked a holy man what prayers or magical incantations he had which would bring her son back to life.

Instead of sending her away or reasoning with her, he said to her, "Fetch me a mustard seed from a home that has never known sorrow. We will use it to drive the sorrow out of your life." The woman set off at once in search of that magical mustard seed. She came first to a splendid mansion, knocked at the door, and said, "I am looking for a home that has never known sorrow. Is this such a place? It is very important to me." They told her, "You've certainly come to the wrong place," and began to describe all the tragic things that had recently befallen them. The woman said to herself, "Who is better able to help these poor unfortunate people than I, who have had misfortune of my own?" She stayed to comfort them, then went on in her search for a home that had never known sorrow. But wherever she turned, in hovels and in palaces, she found one tale after another of sadness and misfortune. Ultimately, she became so involved in ministering to other people's grief that she forgot about her quest for the magical mustard seed, never realizing that it had in fact driven the sorrow out of her life.[3]

Don't let the wailing demands of unmet desire drown out the la-

ments of others, for their hurts may be just the music needed to lift
you above the dirges of self-pity. When unfulfillment seems to have
paralyzed you, precisely then, when you least feel like it, commit
yourself to serving others in some way: visit a shut-in, or teach a
Sunday-school class, or volunteer at a local crisis center, or work for
a worthwhile community cause—do something to help meet a need
outside yourself.

**The Discipline of Giving Yourself to What's at Hand**
Unfulfillment leads us to look toward a future in which our desires
will be met, with the result that we tend to overlook the present.
When we focus on distant horizons of hoped-for fulfillment, we
tend to forget about the ground under our feet.

A woman, for example, longs for a more intimate relationship
than she experiences with her husband; she dreams of a more
romantic mate, a closer friend, a more passionate lover. But fantasies
blind her to the gestures her husband *does* make. If she would spend
as much energy working to strengthen the marriage she has as she
does dreaming about the marriage she wishes she had, her day-to-
day reality would look much more like her dreams.

To use another example, a pastor finds himself in a small church
in which he is the tenor section of the choir, the chief peacemaker
in the Women's Association and the repairman for an antique furnace. It wouldn't take long for God to get his attention to call him
to a "broader" ministry. In fact, the frustrated pastor dreams about
it almost every day; he wishes he were in a place where his gifts
were used more effectively. But thinking too much about different
fields of service might make him neglect the field he's in and leave
the crops unharvested.

Jesus, according to John's Gospel, knew he was bound for glory, but that didn't prevent him from wrapping a towel around his waist, taking a basin in hand and washing dirty feet; it was precisely this attentiveness to concrete problems at hand—no matter how apparently insignificant—which revealed the true nature of his greatness. He lived each day in a way that enabled his Father to echo what Jesus said a pleased master might say to a trustworthy servant: "Well done, good and faithful servant; you have been faithful over a little, I will set you over much; enter into the joy of your master" (Mt 25:21).

During World War II, England needed to increase its production of coal. Winston Churchill called together labor leaders to enlist their support. At the end of his presentation he asked them to picture in their minds a parade which he knew would be held in Picadilly Circus after the war. First, he said, would come the sailors who had kept the vital sea lanes open. Then would come the soldiers who had come home from Dunkirk and then gone on to defeat Rommel in Africa. Then would come the pilots who had driven the Luftwaffe from the sky. Last of all, he said, would come a long line of sweat-stained, soot-streaked men in miner's caps. Someone would cry from the crowd, "And where were you during the critical days of our struggle?" And from ten thousand throats would come the answer, "We were deep in the earth with our faces to the coal."[4]

We might wish for something more exciting than chipping away at the life in front of us, but today's tasks are vital for tomorrow's victory.

One factor increasing restlessness in the mines is the tendency to compare oneself with others; sailors and soldiers and pilots all seem to do so much more, all seem to lead more interesting lives. Professional accomplishments can feel paltry when your fingers get crushed by a young person scrambling up the ladder above you. Or family life can seem shabby after meeting a couple down the block who haven't yet realized the honeymoon's over and have kids with naturally straight teeth, bright minds and happy dispositions, not to mention a purebred dog who always does his business on the compost pile in the back yard. How can you be happy with what you have when others seem to have so much more?

Giving yourself fully to what's at hand demands, therefore, a disciplined refusal to keep score. One good reason not to try to keep score is that you *can't* keep score. You never have all the facts. You might see a person racing ahead of the pack in a career, but do you also see his family life breaking into a million bits because of neglect? You might see someone with a marriage to covet, but do you also see the cancer silently eating away her right breast? The only one with enough information to keep an accurate score is God, and he doesn't flash it on a board for the whole stadium to see.

I used to golf occasionally with an elder in my first church. One day, as we walked together down a long fairway, he said to me, "Now that I'm retired, my wife and I play golf several times a week. And we have the best time. Do you know why? We never keep score. The joy of the game is enough for us."

That's a good way to shoot a round of life, too.

### The Discipline of Patience
Unfulfillment pulls the plug on patience, draining it faster than a jug of iced tea in July. The pain of frustrated desire cries out for immediate relief. When you have a headache, you don't wait a few days before taking an aspirin; when you feel as though you've just eaten half the pizza parlor, you don't wait until next month before drinking antacid. Some things need immediate attention. So when

the emptiness inside feels like you've swallowed a ten-pound brick of raw ache, you want relief—and fast.

Little in our society encourages the cultivation of patience. In the morning I can make a cup of instant coffee to drink as I hurry down the express lane of the freeway to an office where I write on a high-speed word processor before pausing at a drive-through bank window to get money for a pit stop at McDonalds en route to a half-day seminar on being a "one minute manager" that I hope will give me more time with my family after I throw a frozen dinner into the microwave to eat while I watch a thirty minute summary of the world's news. No wonder patience in contemporary America is about as scarce as oxygen on the top of Mt. Everest.

We are obsessed with time. We manage it with appointment calendars, measure it with sophisticated technology and massage its marks out of our faces with high-priced ointments.

Paradoxically, we dread the passing of time but look forward to the future. Yet life happens in the meantime—between memories and hopes, between painful regrets and desperate longings. When unfulfillment afflicts us, the meantime becomes a prison from which we want to escape as soon as yesterday; we think we can't wait—not as children, say, who *think* they can't wait for Christmas, but in the sense that we think we *can't* wait.

The truth about time is this: all time is God's time. He created time, sustains time and has entered time in Jesus Christ to save it from meaninglessness and the absolute timelessness of death. He is, therefore, Lord of time. Your time and my time, past time and future time and the meantime—all times are held in God's loving hands.

That's the good news. The bad news is that his schedule differs from ours. We want things today that God wants to give us tomorrow, or we want to put off until tomorrow what God wants for us today. But God the Father knows best; no caring parent ever operates according to his or her children's timetable. The eternal, omniscient perspective differs radically from our narrow view of things, and therefore we need to learn to trust here, too, the goodness of God.

Donald Bloesch reminds us that "God may delay his answer in order to secure our humble dependence on him. We need to wait for the right time, which is known only to him. It was seven years before William Carey baptized his first convert in India, and it was likewise seven years before Henry Richards gained his first convert in the Congo."[5] If God took that long before granting the worthy requests of these missionaries, we should probably count on having to wait for the fulfillment of some of our desires. We would do well to practice—as we practice any skill, going over the basics again and again and again—the discipline of patience.

## Discussion Questions

1. How is the discipline of accepting incompleteness different from fatalism? Why is incompleteness hard to deal with and difficult to accept?

2. How do you respond to risks? How does the discipline of failing forward help us to take risks? Is there a risk God wants you to take that you are holding back on?

3. Serving others often helps us to cope with our own sorrows. Why do you think this is so? What does this say about who we are and how we ought to live? What are some ways you can put this discipline in practice?

4. Why is it so difficult to stay focused on the present? How can you guard against living in the past or future?

5. When was the last time you felt anxious or stressful? How often do you feel this way? Despite knowing that God is the Lord of time and that he sovereignly oversees our lives, why do we still worry so much? How can we learn the discipline of patience?

# SUNDAY

But all shall be well and all shall be well
and all manner of thing shall be well.
*DAME JULIAN OF NORWICH*

# CHAPTER THIRTEEN

# Beyond
# Positive
# Thinking

**A**rthur *Schlesinger, Jr., in his book* The Cycles of American History, argued that with "the acceleration in the rate of social change, humans become creatures characterized by inextinguishable discontent. . . . Disappointment is the universal modern malady."[1]

This book has attempted to deal honestly with this problem, to recognize, on the one hand, the inevitability and pain of disappointment, and on the other hand, its usefulness as God's tool for the sculpting of our characters into the image of Jesus Christ. And I have tried to show the limited value of positive thinking in helping us cope with this malady; the technique may provide power for some things but never enough to propel us over the gaping pit of unfulfillment.

The news of Good Friday is that God in Christ has entered into the pit with us, bearing our sin and sharing our sorrow. The pain persists but now a Presence graces it. And the news this side of the Cross, the news of Saturday, is that God the Holy Spirit can strengthen us, if we open ourselves to his help by using even unfulfillment to help transform us into better people.

Now this news from two-thirds of the weekend may be good—helpful perhaps—but not *great* news. At best it's ambiguous news, barely gospel. For though the knowledge that we're not alone and that we're growing in our hurt provides encouragement, it still leaves us precisely *in* our hurt. If nothing more could be said about the problem of unfulfillment, I would find the thought that I might die a better person not nearly comforting enough to keep me from falling into hopelessness: I would find it hard to disagree with Ernest Becker's conclusion that "what has been taking place on the planet for about three billion years is that it is being turned into a vast pit of fertilizer,"[2] and as a consequence I would find myself consuming more than my share of the twenty-eight tons of aspirin, tranquilizers and sleeping pills Americans take every day to escape from the stress of living.[3]

But we are not left with this Saturday existence. Thank God, tomorrow is Sunday. The message of Easter startles us from the nightmare of despair with a trumpet blast of hope announcing a new dawn.

Our culture knows little of hope. It speaks much of optimism and positive thinking, but loses its tongue when asked about hope. When the subject is discussed, it's usually weighted with enough doubt to sink it in a sea of despair, such as Bertrand Russell's honest confession:

> The center of me is always and eternally a terrible pain—a curious, wild pain—a searching for something beyond what the world contains, something transfigured and infinite, the beatific vision—God. I do not find it, I do not think it is to be found, but the love of it is my life; it's like passionate love for a ghost. At times it fills me with rage, at times with wild despair; it is the source of gentleness and cruelty and work; it fills every passion I have. It is the actual spring of life in me.[4]

These sad words are filled with intense longing. But with hope? Russell reaches only for a ghost which disappears in the embrace; he desperately wants something but believes in nothing—a literal Nothing which awaits his passionate desire.

The Christian's hope, too, is often "a curious, wild pain," but it embraces more than a ghost; it clings to the resurrected Christ. "We have been born anew to a living hope through the resurrection of Jesus Christ from the dead" (1 Pet 1:3). Hermann Hesse was wrong when he wrote: "We have to stumble through so much dirt . . . before we reach home. And we have no one to guide us. Our only guide is our homesickness."[5] Indeed, there is much dirt through which we must stumble, but we have more to guide us than subjective feelings of homesickness. We have before us a person alive with the eternal love of God who says, "Follow me, for I know the way to the fulfillment of your deepest longings."

### God's Laugh

In the ancient Russian Orthodox tradition, the day after Easter was devoted to telling jokes. Why would priests and people sit around a table all day saying, "Have you heard the one about . . ."? "This was the way, they felt, that they were imitating the cosmic joke that

God pulled on Satan in the resurrection. Satan thought he had won, and was smug in his victory, smiling to himself, having the last word. So he thought. Then God raised up Jesus from the dead, and life and salvation became the last words."[6]

In the resurrection of Jesus Christ God had the last laugh, so to speak, and we are still laughing with him. In Eugene O'Neill's play *Lazarus Laughed* the crowd asks Lazarus, after he emerged from the tomb, "What is beyond?" Lazarus responds, "There is only life! I heard the heart of Jesus laughing in my heart. . . . And my heart reborn to love and life cried 'Yes' and I laughed in the laughter of God!" Later in the play he describes himself in the tomb: "Then, of a sudden, a strange gay laughter trembled from his heart as though his life, so long repressed in him by fear, had at last found its voice and a song for singing."[7]

The great news of Easter is that the life within us, sick with longing and often buried in despair, can at last find its voice and a song to sing. For the story is not over.

Some years ago I saw a picture hanging in the nave of St. Paul's Cathedral. It was taken during the London blitz. A smoky darkness filled most of the picture, except the center, where a courageous ray of sunlight had pierced through the horror to illumine the beautiful dome of St. Paul's. The resurrection is like that shaft of light; it shines back on the cross and reveals its meaning. In Easter's light we see things we could not have seen before. The dawn of eternal day dispels the darkness of Friday and the disorienting fog of Saturday. What we see is this: the affirmation of one who had been abandoned for our sake.

Jesus Christ entered fully into our brokenness, taking even our sin upon himself, and was therefore handed over to the godforsakenness we deserve; the Son rejected by the Father. But this rupture of trinal unity, this "death in God," was not the final revelation of God. The abandonment of Friday, though horrific beyond our under-standing, was overcome by the greater affirmation of Sunday. Death was taken into the being of God and thus surrounded by the life of God. The no of Friday, which we must hear in all its terror as the word of God's wrath against our sin, was on Sunday shown to be part of a louder, gracious yes.

The resurrection validated the ministry of Jesus, creating a dra-matic reversal. It revealed that he "died as a righteous man, not as a blasphemer. Rather, those who rejected him as a blasphemer and had complicity in his death were the real blasphemers. His judges rightly deserved the punishment that he received. Thus he bore their punishment."[8]

God, in raising Jesus from death, said yes to this unexpected turn of events. He accepted the death of the innocent one as the death of the guilty ones. Jesus' victory then became the blasphemers' vic-tory, too; having died with him they can also live with him. This is what filled the apostles with such explosive joy, for they saw in their Master's resurrection the promise of their own resurrection. "Christ has been raised from the dead, the first fruits of those who have fallen asleep. . . . For as in Adam all die, so also in Christ shall all be made alive. But each in his own order: Christ the first fruits, then at his coming those who belong to Christ" (1 Cor 15:20-23).

So with O'Neill's Lazarus, our life, long repressed by fear—fear of living and dying with unfulfillment—can at last find its voice and a song to sing. We are born again. As a mother delivers her baby from the darkness of the womb into the fullness of human life, Jesus' resurrection delivers us into a new order of existence, a life drawing its breath from the promise of God's yes, a life with a heart of hope pulsating with the unfailing rhythm of God's eternal laughter.

**Restlessness as a Witness**

Nothing in this life ever really satiates our hunger; at most, temporary relief is occasionally found but it never lasts long. Christian hope is more than the usual desire coming from unfulfillment. Authentic hope can be created only by something that breaks into the normal cause and effect processes of our history with the freedom of God himself, something that blows open the front door of our minds to let us look out onto new horizons of possibility. That something is the resurrection of Jesus Christ from death. The holy God presents himself to us in this event as the God of a new future, a future marked not by the brokenness of our sin but by the wholeness of his salvation.

Still, simple human desire should not be despised. It has an important function. Though it can't lead us home, it can witness to the existence of a home which gives rise to our homesickness in the first place. The experience of unfulfilled longing speaks to us, if we let it, of an ultimate fulfillment, of something beyond the seemingly endless cycle of temporary relief and disappointment.

Viewed from this perspective, restless desire is certainly not wrong. It can lead into all manner of sinful pursuits and result in painful brokenness, but in itself it points beyond these things. If the veil of misperception were pulled back so that we could see with clarity into the heart of the longing in our hearts, we would see a desire for God, a desire for the fullness of joy that will be ours when we enter his eternal presence.

Of course we don't often see this. We think we want other things—material objects, positions of power, religious experiences—but what we really want is heaven. C. S. Lewis wrote:

There have been times when I think we do not desire heaven but more often I find myself wondering whether, in our heart of hearts, we have ever desired anything else. . . . All the things that have ever deeply possessed your soul have been but hints of it—tantalizing glimpses, promises never quite fulfilled, echoes that died away just as they caught your ear. But if it should really become manifest—if there ever came an echo that did not die away but swelled into the sound itself—you would know it. Beyond all possibility of doubt you would say "Here at last is the thing I was made for."[9]

Unfortunately, we too often confuse the echoes for the sound itself. We err not because we want more but because we want too little.

Indeed, if we consider the unblushing promises of reward and the staggering nature of the rewards promised in the Gospels, it would seem that Our Lord finds our desires not too strong, but too weak. We are half-hearted creatures, fooling about with drink and sex and ambition when infinite joy is offered us. Like an ignorant child who wants to go on making mud pies in a slum because he cannot imagine what is meant by the offer of a holiday at the sea, we are far too easily pleased.[10]

Thus Harry Blamires contends that "unsatisfied longings must be nourished in us, and the elusive dream of fulfillment dangled before us, or we should never know that we are not here, on earth, in our proper resting-place. Utterly divested of this disturbing inheritance . . . hearts would never desire the ultimate peace and joy offered by God."[11] We must let ourselves feel the pain, in other words, and not anesthetize the longing with drugs which inevitably wear off and leave us scrambling for another short-term fix.

### Pie in the Sky

"To play great music," said the violinist Yehudi Menuhin, "you must keep your eyes on a distant star." The resurrection of Jesus Christ is the star toward which we must focus; it is God's promise that the chapter we're now living through is not the end of the story. A final chapter has yet to unfold, in which, as in a fairy tale, the most impossible things will happen. The holy God, whose embrace we have already felt in Jesus Christ, will bring his love to fulfillment. The lost will be found; the broken will be made whole; prodigals will get drunk on the wine of the Father's pleasure. All joys we have ever known, from the ordinary delights of being human to the freedom of God's grace, will be shown to be first blushes on the horizon of an as yet unimagined dawn.

The Scriptures describe the new existence promised through Christ's resurrection in a variety of ways: the kingdom of God, eternal life, heaven, a new heaven and a new earth, the holy city, new Jerusalem, the Father's house, glory, our inheritance, the prize of the upward call of God in Christ Jesus. Though each of these conveys a different nuance in the biblical narrative, they point to a common reality—God's salvation, the victory of his life over sin's death. We are not given exact details of this new life, but we are told that it will more than compensate for earthly sorrows. "I consider that the sufferings of this present time are not worth comparing with the glory that is to be revealed," Paul wrote to Christians in Rome (Rom 8:18). And in the Corinthian correspondence he said something similar, with an added dimension: "For this slight momentary affliction is preparing for us an eternal weight of glory beyond all comparison" (2 Cor 4:17). The affliction of the moment, which will be nothing next to the glory of eternity, is in some way even now preparing us for that glory.

Now this might strike the critic as simply "pie in the sky," an evasion of painful reality. But as C. S. Lewis pointed out, "either there is 'pie in the sky' or there is not. If there is not, then Christianity is false, for this doctrine is woven into its whole fabric. If there is, then this truth, like any other, must be faced, whether it is useful at political meetings or no."[12] When we do listen carefully to the news announced in this doctrine, we hear a message of comfort and hope which keeps us moving through the distresses of unfulfillment.

Whether or not ideas of eternity involve a flight from the problems of earthly life depends entirely on the origin of those ideas. If they arise out of our own subjective longings, they may indeed be an attempt to pave an avenue of escape from this world. If, on the other hand, they come to us from an objective event outside us—the resurrection of Jesus Christ from death—the way of escape is forever blocked. For the risen Lord in whom we hope is none other than the one who came and is coming again to *this* world.

### Worldliness for Christ's Sake

Christian hope is not other-worldly but profoundly this-worldly. The word *world* is used in two ways in Scripture. It sometimes refers to the pattern of living marked by sin and doomed to pass away by God's grace, as in the admonition, "Do not love the world or the things in the world" (1 Jn 2:15). But it is also used in a very different sense. "God so loved the world," we are told, "that he gave his only Son, that whoever believes in him should not perish but have eternal life. For God sent the Son into the world, not to condemn the world, but that the world might be saved through him" (Jn 3:16-17).

God has a passionate love affair with this world, and he is not yet finished with it; his act of grace in Christ was no temporary fling but an eternal commitment. The one who came into the world to die for its sins will return, bringing with him the consummation of God's salvation. The disciples who witnessed Christ's ascension were not allowed to stand gazing into the sky but were told, "This Jesus, who was taken up from you into heaven, will come in the same way as you saw him go into heaven" (Acts 1:11). The meaning was clear: because the Lord is not yet finished with this world, neither may his followers say "to hell with it all" but must say with their lives "to heaven with it all."

While running a few years ago I saw a couple of joggers coming toward me. One of them, I noticed, was gripping with one hand the arm of his companion and with the other the distinctive white cane of a blind person. As they passed by I saw that the blind jogger was around seventy years old. That's commitment. A man with an old, broken body—but a body still, and worth caring for—refusing to give up on it.

And neither may we give up on life in this world. It may not be all we'd like, and it may be filled with enough pain to make us wonder if it's worth carrying on, but it's still the life God declared "good" at creation and redeemed in Christ. We must not break faith with our Lord by turning our backs on something he loves. Yes, we look forward to more than this world provides; in the meantime, however, we take our places in it, fully engaged with its joys and sorrows and longings. We know something the world doesn't yet know about itself: it is God's and he has staked his claim to it through the incarnation of his Son.

Therefore, we may hope not simply for ourselves but for the future of all that is good in this life. God will not allow the destruction of his creation; he remains unreservedly committed to it. "The creation itself will be set free from its bondage to decay and obtain the glorious liberty of the children of God" (Rom 8:21). We may thus serve creation—preserving life, establishing relationships, protecting the environment, seeking social justice, beautifying through art and enriching our worldly existence however we can—and know that ultimately nothing we do will be wasted.

I believe that nothing good in life will be lost. Transformed, yes, but not lost. The body of our Lord, though changed by the resurrection into a higher order of existence (after Easter, Jesus could apparently appear or disappear at will), maintained continuity with the earthly body which preceded it (the disciples recognized Jesus as they ate breakfast with him one morning by the Sea of Galilee). The experiences of this life will in the same way be transformed but not lost. So a blind seventy-year-old had better stay committed to his body, and for that matter might as well start taking lessons in conversational Russian too. And we all ought to keep investing ourselves in those endeavors which from an earthly perspective seem to offer little hope of reward for our labors. I'm reminded of the delightful story about the great cellist Pablo Cassals. When he was ninety he continued to practice four to five hours every day. When asked why, he answered, "Because I have the impression I am making progress."[13] We're all making progress whether we realize it or not.

"To accept this world as a destination rather than a staging post," wrote Malcolm Muggeridge, "would seem to me to reduce life to something too banal and trivial to be taken seriously or held in esteem."[14] Indeed, for to have Nothing awaiting all things would be like a black hole sucking all present meaning into its void. But if Glory will someday seize this world, shaking it free from the dust of death, it is even now lifted to an indestructible significance.

The resurrection of Christ should radically change our view of the world, and the part of the world toward which we need most radically to change our perspective is humanity itself. Paul, when reflecting on the love of Christ, wrote, "From now on, therefore, we

regard no one from a human point of view" (2 Cor 5:16). C. S. Lewis
pointed out:

> It is a serious thing to live in a society of possible gods and
> goddesses, to remember that the dullest and most uninteresting
> person you talk to may one day be a creature which, if you saw
> it now, you would be strongly tempted to worship, or else a horror
> and a corruption such as you now meet, if at all, only in a
> nightmare. All day long we are, in some degree, helping each
> other to one or other of these destinations. It is in the light of
> these overwhelming possibilities, it is with the awe and the cir-
> cumspection proper to them, that we should conduct all our
> dealings with one another, all friendships, all loves, all play, all
> politics. There are no *ordinary* people.[15]

Contrary to popular sentiment, hope in Christ is not escapist. Rather, our faith sends us back into the world as ambassadors of the
coming kingdom. Precisely because we hope for something more we
have the energy to keep living in the present. While the German
Air Force rained terror on the City of London during the fall of 1940,
with an average of two hundred planes per raid for fifty-seven
consecutive nights, Winston Churchill could be seen picking his
way through the devastation, dressed in suit and derby and chomp-
ing his ever-present cigar, encouraging the Londoners he met. Victory eventually came for Great Britain, of course, and when it did
Churchill was asked what he had done during the interminable
nights of the London bombing. He responded that he had gone to
his bomb shelter below Piccadilly Circus and there, with a desk
lamp illuminating a map of Europe, had planned the invasion of
Germany.[16] Because we, too, are confident of victory, we can stra-
tegize and work for it even while surrounded by the chaos of the
present brokenness.

## The View from the Mountaintop

Being worldly for Christ's sake does not mean losing sight of heaven. We must affirm life but not cling to it. Because our *present* experiences will be redeemed, we may take hold of them enthusiastically; because our present experiences will be *redeemed,* we must take hold of them lightly. This provides the freedom necessary to serve this world with joy.

Have you ever had to part from a friend you knew you'd probably never see again? The last conversation becomes awkward. Knowing it is the end, you attempt to squeeze every minute of time for all it's worth, with the result that it isn't worth much. Desperation strangles freedom. How different from the conversations that created the relationship, conversations that became more meaningful as freedom increased!

If we believe this life is all we have, we will feel no option but to reach for all the gusto we can, and that grasping will inevitably choke the joy out of life. We will not be able to keep our eyes off what escapes our grip and what falls through our fingers (we can hold only so much, after all), and the pain of unfulfillment will intensify. There will never be enough time and energy and opportunity to satisfy our hunger for . . . what? For the Joy that is really God himself. We will become like athletes who know they are playing a losing game, defeated by the deadly duo of desire and hopelessness.

And it's no consolation to imagine yourself living on in the memory of your loved ones. Woody Allen, in an interview with *Rolling Stone* magazine was being realistic when he said, "Someone once asked me if my dream was to live on in the hearts of my people, and I said I would like to live on in my apartment. And that's really what I would prefer. . . . You drop dead one day, and it means less than nothing if billions of people are singing your praises every day, all day long."[17] Better to experience for yourself all you can before the curtain falls, if this really is your last scene in the last act of the last play. But who can experience enough to be free from desperation? To live peacefully in such circumstances requires either the anesthesia of apathy or an acting performance worthy of an Academy Award.

However, if we are playing a part not in a tragedy but in a never-ending fairy tale, which will have the most impossible, joy-filled twists in the drama, we can say our lines with freedom and joy. We can accept the incompleteness of our lives without desperation. We can serve our world without calculating costs.

On the evening before an assassin's bullet lethally ripped into his body, Martin Luther King, Jr., said to a crowd of two thousand gathered at the Clayborn Temple in Memphis, Tennessee:

> I don't know what will happen to me now. We've got some difficult days ahead. But it really doesn't matter to me now. Because I've been to the mountaintop. I won't mind.
>
> Like anybody else, I would like to live a long life. Longevity has its place. But I'm not concerned about that now. I just want to do God's will. And he's allowed me to go up to the mountain. And I've looked over, and I've seen the Promised Land.
>
> I may not get there with you, but I want you to know that we as a people will get to the Promised Land.
>
> So I'm happy tonight. I'm not worried about anything. I'm not fearing any man. Mine eyes have seen the glory of the coming of the Lord.[18]

The resurrection of Jesus Christ is the mountaintop from which we have viewed the Promised Land. We have seen a place where our present experiences will be set free from the ambiguities of unfulfillment; we have recognized a light burning in the window, and like travelers, weary with the cold and darkness but pushing on because of homesickness, we have caught a second wind and felt our hearts lifting in anticipated joy; we have had the first glimpses of glory. Seeing this Promised Land and knowing that we *will* get there frees us to live without fear.

### From the Shadow of Death to the Light of Life

The final experience of unfulfillment we must all face is the most radical of all: death. Viewed from the perspective of this life it is absolute negation, the triumph of incompleteness. But from the mountaintop of Christ's resurrection it looks very different. It is the river Jordan, as the old spirituals imagined, through which we must pass on our way into the Promised Land. The river may be deep and wide, chilling the body and even the soul, but God's promise delivered through the prophet of old is for us, too: "Fear not, for I have redeemed you; I have called you by name, you are mine. When you pass through the waters I will be with you; and through the rivers, they shall not overwhelm you" (Is 43:1-2).

A German sailor once wrote to his mother: "If you should hear our cruiser has been sunk and that no one has been saved, do not weep. The sea in which my body sinks is also the hollow of the hand of my Savior, from which nothing can separate me." The apostle Paul, writing centuries before, had the same conviction: "For I am sure that neither death, nor life, nor angels, nor principalities, nor things present, nor things to come, nor powers, nor height, nor depth, nor anything else in all creation, will be able to separate us from the love of God in Christ Jesus our Lord" (Rom 8:38-39).

Dietrich Bonhoeffer's life and death has had a great impact on many in our time. He was a brilliant young student of theology, reared in an upper-middle class German home with all the cultural advantages of the bourgeois; he established a solid academic reputation, pastored for a time in London and Barcelona, and traveled widely on behalf of the ecumenical movement—including a study and lecture tour of the United States; he struggled to maintain the integrity of a church torn asunder by the pressures of National Socialism, directed an underground seminary, joined the resistance against Hitler, and was finally hanged as a conspirator, at the age of thirty-nine, during the last days of the war. No wonder Kenneth Hamilton observed that "it is the life as much as the thought of Dietrich Bonhoeffer that has caught the imagination of men of our age and made him so central a figure in the contemporary theological scene."[19]

While in prison Bonhoeffer wrote a poem, "Powers of Good," in which he affirmed his trust in the providence of God: "Should it be ours to drain the cup of grieving/ even to the dregs of pain, at thy command,/ we will not falter, thankfully receiving/ all that is given by thy loving hand."[20] A few months later, on April 9, 1945, he was taken to the gallows. Bonhoeffer's last words were to Payne Best, a British officer who had a room across the corridor from his. He asked him to pass a message to his trusted friend Bishop Bell: "Tell him that for me this is the end, but also the beginning."[21]

The beginning. So the last picture we have of Bonhoeffer is a man naked under the scaffold, kneeling to pray. Five minutes later he was dead. And alive.

A new beginning is what the resurrection of Jesus Christ promises. Then shall be fully realized the biblical declaration, "If anyone is in Christ, he is a new creation; the old has passed away, behold, the new has come" (2 Cor 5:17).

We shall *be* new and therefore we shall *see* anew. When Sunday's light dawns, all shall be clear. "For now we see in a mirror dimly, but then face to face" (1 Cor 13:12). In the presence of God—Joy Absolute—we shall see that the unfulfillment in our hearts was for much more than we could ever have dreamed. We shall see that surrounding all our restless strivings—our desperate attempts to satisfy our longings with the gods of materialism, power and religion, and our futile attempts to haul ourselves over mountains of difficulties with hard work and positive thinking—have been arms of eternal love, carrying us to Fulfillment. We shall see that the God of Jesus Christ, in whom we have had a faith sometimes strong and sometimes weak, has always been with us, offering the grace of Good Friday and strength for Saturday. All this shall be clear. And "all shall be well and all shall be well and all manner of thing shall be well."

## Discussion Questions

1. As a culture, what are some of the things we place our hope in? How does what we hope for affect the way we live?

2. C. S. Lewis notes that "our Lord finds our desires not too strong, but too weak." What are your deepest longings and desires? In what ways are they "too weak"?

3. Knowing that the kingdom of God is at hand and that its consummation is coming, how should this affect how we approach our work, our friendships, how we spend our time and so on?

4. How do we balance love for the world with the danger of becoming too worldly? What are some practical ways this balance can be worked out in your life?

5. Seeing this Promised Land and knowing that we *will* get there frees us to live without fear. How does this knowledge help us when we face the feelings of unfulfillment and restlessness and the many disappointments of this life?

# Notes

### Chapter 1: When Can-Do Can't
[1]The names in this story have been changed.
[2]Julien Green, *God's Fool—The Life and Times of Francis of Assisi,* trans. Peter Heinegg (San Francisco: Harper and Row, 1985), p. 63.
[3]Oswald Chambers, "Where God Hides His Glory," *Christianity Today,* November 8, 1985, p. 29.

### Chapter 2: Can-Do Culture
[1]Watty Piper, *The Little Engine That Could* (New York: Platt & Munk, 1976).
[2]Douglas John Hall, *Lighten Our Darkness: Toward an Indigenous Theology of the Cross* (Philadelphia: Westminster Press, 1976), p. 39.
[3]As quoted in Daniel J. Boorstin, *The Americans: The Colonial Experience* (New York: Vintage Books, 1958), p. 3.
[4]Ibid., p. 5.
[5]Robert N. Bellah et al., *Habits of the Heart: Individualism and Commitment in American Life* (Berkeley: University of California Press, 1985), p. 32.
[6]Malcolm R. Eiselen, "Benjamin Franklin," *The World Book Encyclopedia,* Vol. 7 (Chicago: World Book, 1983), p. 413.
[7]Tom Wolfe, *The Purple Decades* (New York: Berkley Books, 1982), pp. 291, 293.
[8]See Christopher Lasch, *The Culture of Narcissism* (New York: Warner Books, 1979).

### Chapter 3: Can-Do Faith
[1]D. M. Baillie, *God Was in Christ* (New York: Charles Scribner's Sons, 1948), pp.

205-6.

[2]James M. Gustafson, *Ethics from a Theocentric Perspective, Vol. 1: Theology and Ethics* (Chicago: University of Chicago Press, 1981), p. 18.

[3]Gloria Copeland, *God's Will Is Prosperity* (Fort Worth: KCP Publications, 1978).

**Chapter 4: Confessing the Limits**

[1]Abraham Maslow, *Motivation and Personality* (New York: Harper and Row, 1970), p. 46.

[2]Dominique Lapierre, *The City of Joy,* trans. Kathryn Spink (New York: Doubleday, 1985), pp. 41-42.

[3]Tom Callahan, "Life's Not a Bowl of Any Single Thing," *Time,* January 27, 1986, p. 53.

[4]C. Stephen Evans, "The Blessings of Mental Anguish," *Christianity Today,* January 17, 1986, p. 29.

[5]Jacques Ellul, *Hope in Time of Abandonment,* trans. C. Edward Hopkin (New York: Seabury Press, 1973), p. 3.

[6]Harry Emerson Fosdick, *Hope of the World* (New York: Harper and Row, 1933), p.190.

[7]Malcolm Muggeridge, *The Green Stick* (New York: William Morrow, 1973), p.17.

**Chapter 5: False Gods: Materialism, Power and Religion**

[1]Robert Heilbroner, "Advertising as Agitprop—Puncturing Myths about Hype," *Harpers,* January 1985, p. 72.

[2]As quoted in Karl Menninger, *Whatever Became of Sin?* (New York: Dutton, 1973), pp. 151-52.

[3]Herbert Schlossberg, *Idols for Destruction* (Nashville: Thomas Nelson, 1983), p.197.

[4]Jerald C. Brauer, ed., "Friedrich Wilhelm Nietzsche," *The Westminster Dictionary of Church History* (Philadelphia: Westminster Press, 1971), p. 603.

[5]Colin Brown, "The Ascent of Man," *Eerdman's Handbook to the History of Christianity,* ed. Tim Dowley (Grand Rapids: Eerdmans, 1977) p. 543.

[6]Karl Barth, *Church Dogmatics,* Vol. 4, pt. 1, trans. G. W. Bromiley (Edinburgh: T.& T. Clark, 1956), p. 262.

[7]Ibid. p. 263.

[8]Ibid. pp. 263-64.

[9]Paul Brand with Philip Yancey, "A Surgeon's View of Divine Healing," *Christianity Today,* November 25, 1983, p. 15.

[10]Joseph A. Fitzmeyer, *The Gospel According to Luke I-IX* (Garden City, N.Y.: Doubleday, 1981), p. 517.

## Chapter 6: The View from the Sanctuary

[1]Emile Cailliet, *Pascal: Genius in the Light of Scripture* (Philadelphia: Westminster Press, 1945), p. 131.
[2]Charles Williams, *The Place of the Lion* (Grand Rapids: Eerdmans, 1974), pp. 74-75.
[3]Annie Dillard, *Holy the Firm* (Bantam, 1977), p. 60.
[4]O. Procksch, "αγιο6," *Theological Dictionary of the New Testament,* Vol. 1, ed. Gerhard Kittel, trans. Geoffrey Bromiley (Grand Rapids: Eerdmans, 1964), p. 89.
[5]Walther Eichrodt, *Theology of the Old Testaments,* Vol. 1, trans. J. A. Baker (Philadelphia: Westminster Press, 1961), p. 270.
[6]Gerhard von Rad, *Old Testament Theology,* Vol. 1, trans. D. M. G. Stalker (New York: Harper and Row, 1962), p. 205.
[7]Kenneth Grahame, *The Wind in the Willows* (London: Methuen Children's Books, Magnet reprint ed., 1978), pp. 134-35.
[8]Annie Dillard, *Teaching a Stone to Talk* (New York: Harper and Row, 1982), pp. 41-42.

## Chapter 7: A Refining Fire

[1]C. S. Lewis, *The Lion, the Witch, and the Wardrobe* (London: Puffin, 1950), p. 75.
[2]Helmut Thielicke, *Theological Ethics: Foundations,* ed. William H. Lazareth (Grand Rapids: Eerdmans, 1979), p. 98.
[3]Brennan Manning, *The Wisdom of Accepted Tenderness: Going Deeper into the Abba Experience* (Denville, N.J.: Dimension Books, 1978), pp. 50-52.

## Chapter 8: The Difference Friday Makes

[1]Robert Farrar Capon, *Between Noon and Three* (San Francisco: Harper and Row, 1982), pp. 114-15.
[2]Lewis B. Smedes, "Preaching to Ordinary People," *Leadership,* Fall 1983, p. 119.
[3]Barth, *Church Dogmantics,* Vol. 4, pt. 1, p. xx.
[4]I am indebted to Helmut Thielicke for my understanding of this text. See Thielicke, *Theological Ethics: Foundations,* pp. 258-59.
[5]Paul Tillich, *The Shaking of the Foundations* (Middlesex: Penguin, 1962), p. 163.
[6]Lewis B. Smedes, *How Can It Be All Right When Everything Is All Wrong?* (San Francisco: Harper and Row, 1982), p. 115.

## Chapter 9: Never Alone

[1]Elie Wiesel, *Night* (New York: Bantam, 1960), pp. 72-73.
[2]Dorothy L. Sayers, *Creed or Chaos?* (New York: Harcourt, Brace, 1949), p. 4.

[3]G. C. Berkouwer, for example, argues that both *patripassianism* (the suffering of the Father) and *theopaschitism* (the suffering of God) are ideas "at the periphery of the church," which cause a "mutilation of the mystery of the trinity." He wants to maintain the necessary distinction between Father, Son and Holy Spirit—an important caution, to be sure (G. C. Berkouwer, *The Work of Christ,* trans. Cornelius Lambregtse [Grand Rapids: Eerdmans, 1965], pp. 265, 279). But he overstates his case and undercuts the equally important truth of the unity of the Godhead. Perhaps we should not speak about the suffering of the Father, in order to differentiate clearly between the first and second persons of the Trinity. (What father, though, would not in some sense suffer with the death of a beloved son?) Surely we must, however, speak of the suffering of God if we would accurately interpret the death of him who was true man and true God.

[4]Jürgen Moltmann, *The Trinity and the Kingdom,* trans. Margaret Kohl (San Francisco: Harper and Row, 1981), p. 23.

[5]Wiesel, *Night,* pp. 61-62.

[6]Jürgen Moltmann, *The Crucified God,* trans. R. A. Wilson and John Bowden (New York: Harper and Row, 1974), p. 227.

[7]Eberhard Busch, "My Memories of Karl Barth," *Reformed Journal,* May 1986, p. 14.

[8]Martin Marty, *A Cry of Absence: Reflections for the Winter of the Heart* (San Francisco: Harper and Row, 1983), p. 139.

**Chapter 10: The Good News of Brokenness**

[1]As quoted by Madeleine L'Engle, *Walking on Water: Reflections on Faith and Art* (New York: Bantam, 1982), p. 26.

[2]Paul Tournier, *Creative Suffering,* trans. Edwin Hudson (San Francisco: Harper and Row, 1982), p. 98.

[3]Ibid., p. 2.

[4]Ibid., pp. 4-13.

[5]As quoted in Eugene Peterson, *Run with the Horses* (Downers Grove, Ill.: InterVarsity Press, 1983), p. 192.

[6]Ibid. pp. 83-84.

[7]As quoted in Charles Cummings, *The Mystery of the Ordinary* (San Francisco: Harper and Row, 1982), p. 120.

[8]Ibid.

[9]C. S. Lewis, *The Problem of Pain* (New York: Macmillan, 1962), p. 93.

[10]Quoted in ibid., p. 96.

[11]Frederick Dale Bruner, *A Theology of the Holy Spirit* (Grand Rapids: Eerdmans, 1970), p. 304.

¹²Ibid., p. 305.

## Chapter 11: Disciplines for Living with God
¹Quoted in John R. Wimmer, *No Pain, No Gain* (New York: Ballantine, 1985), p. 7.
²Calvin Stapert, "The Statutes of Liberty: Freedom and Law in the Music of Bach," *Reformed Journal*, March 1985, p. 12.
³Karl Barth, *Wolfgang Amadeus Mozart*, trans. Clarence K. Pott (Grand Rapids: Eerdmans, 1986), p. 46.
⁴Harry Emerson Fosdick, *The Meaning of Prayer* (New York: Association Press, 1916), p. 65.
⁵Donald G. Bloesch, *The Struggle of Prayer* (San Francisco: Harper and Row, 1980), p. 7.
⁶Dietrich Bonhoeffer, *Christology*, trans. Edwin Robinson (London: Collins, Fount Paperbacks, 1978), p. 51.
⁷Mark Twain, *Huckleberry Finn* (New York: Penguin, 1966), p. 297.
⁸F. Dale Bruner, "A Tale of Two Sons," *Christianity Today*, October 1985, p. 47.
⁹Freeman Patterson, *Photography and the Art of Seeing* (Philadelphia: Chilton Books, 1965), p. 9.
¹⁰Ernest T. Campbell, *Locked in a Room with Open Doors* (Waco: Word Books, 1974), pp. 30-31.
¹¹John Claypool, *Tracks of a Fellow Struggler: How to Handle Grief* (Waco: Word Books, 1974), pp. 76-77.
¹²Dietrich Bonhoeffer, *Life Together*, trans. John Doberstein (London: SCM Press, 1949), p. 17.
¹³Frederick Buechner, *Peculiar Treasures: A Biblical Who's Who* (San Francisco: Harper and Row, 1979), p. 153.

## Chapter 12: Disciplines for Living in a Broken World
¹Peterson, *Run with the Horses*, pp. 202-3.
²*Bits and Pieces*, April 1986, pp. 21-22.
³Harold Kushner, *When Bad Things Happen to Good People* (New York: Schocken Books, 1981), pp. 110-11.
⁴I am indebted to Allen D. Montgomery for this story, but I can no longer find the source.
⁵Bloesch, *Struggle of Prayer*, p. 91.

## Chapter 13: Beyond Positive Thinking
¹Arthur M. Schlesinger, Jr., *The Cycles of American History* (Boston: Houghton Mif-

flin, 1986), pp. 27-28.

[2]Ernest Becker, *The Denial of Death,* p. 283, as quoted in Smedes, *How Can It Be All Right?* p. 132.

[3]From "To Illustrate," *Preaching,* January-February 1987, p. 53.

[4]I have been unable to find the source for this quotation from Bertrand Russell.

[5]As quoted in David Neff, "Going Home to the Hidden God," *Christianity Today,* April 4, 1986, p. 31.

[6]William J. Bausch, *Storytelling: Imagination and Faith* (Mystic, Conn.: Twenty-Third Publications, 1984), p. 138.

[7]Eugene O'Neill, *Lazarus Laughed* (New York: Boni & Liveright, 1927), pp. 22, 71.

[8]Wolfhart Pannenberg, *Jesus: God and Man,* trans. Lewis L. Wilkins and Duane A. Priebe (London: SCM Press, 1968), p. 259.

[9]Lewis, *Problem of Pain,* pp. 145-46.

[10]C. S. Lewis, *The Weight of Glory* (New York: Macmillan, 1980), pp. 3-4.

[11]Harry Blamires, *The Christian Mind* (Ann Arbor: Servant Books, 1963), pp. 179-80.

[12]Lewis, *Problem of Pain,* pp. 144-45.

[13]Karl Barth, *A Late Friendship—The Letters of Karl Barth and Carl Zuckmayer,* trans. Geoffrey W. Bromiley (Grand Rapids: Eerdmans, 1982), p. 21.

[14]Muggeridge, *Green Stick,* p. 18.

[15]Lewis, *Weight of Glory,* pp. 18-19.

[16]James R. Edwards, "Faith as Noun and Verb," *Christianity Today,* August 9, 1985, p. 23.

[17]Woody Allen, "Interview," *Rolling Stone,* April 9, 1987, p. 88.

[18]Martin Luther King, Jr., as quoted by Coretta Scott King, *My Life with Martin Luther King, Jr.* (London: Hodder & Stoughton Ltd., 1969), p. 328.

[19]Kenneth Hamilton, *Life in One's Stride: A Short Study in Dietrich Bonhoeffer* (Grand Rapids: Eerdmans, 1968), p. 9.

[20]Dietrich Bonhoeffer, *Letters and Papers from Prison,* ed. Eberhard Bethge, trans. Reginald Fuller et al. (London: SCM Press, 1971), p. 400.

[21]Eberhard Bethge, *Dietrich Bonhoeffer,* trans. Eric Mosbacher et al. (London: Collins, Fountain Books, 1977), p. 830.